Our Best Seasonal
QUILTS

from Fons and Porter's
For the Love of Quilting **magazine**

Our Best Seasonal Quilts

From Fons and Porter's *For the Love of Quilting* magazine
©2000 by Oxmoor House, Inc.
Book Division of Southern Progress Corporation
P.O. Box 2463, Birmingham, Alabama 35201

Published by Oxmoor House, Inc., and Leisure Arts, Inc.

Library of Congress Catalog Card Number: 99-76797
ISBN: 0-8487-2362-7
Printed in the United States of America
Third Printing 2001

Editor-in-Chief: Nancy Fitzpatrick Wyatt
Senior Crafts Editor: Susan Ramey Cleveland
Senior Editor, Copy and Homes: Olivia Kindig Wells
Art Director: James Boone

Our Best Seasonal Quilts

From Fons and Porter's *For the Love of Quilting* magazine

Editors: Catherine Corbett Fowler, Rhonda Richards
Copy Editor: L. Amanda Owens
Editorial Assistant: Suzanne Powell
Associate Art Director: Cynthia R. Cooper
Designers: Melissa Jones Clark, Carol Damsky
Illustrator: Kelly Davis
Senior Photographer: John O'Hagan
Photo Stylist: Linda Baltzell Wright
Director, Production and Distribution: Phillip Lee
Associate Production Manager: Theresa L. Beste
Production Assistant: Faye Porter Bonner

Contributors
Technical Writer: Laura Morris Edwards
Pattern Tester: Patricia Everman Myers
Photographer: Keith Harrelson

We're Here for You!

We at Oxmoor House are dedicated to serving you with reliable information that expands your imagination and enriches your life. We welcome your comments and suggestions. Please write us at:

Oxmoor House
Editor, **Our Best Seasonal Quilts**
2100 Lakeshore Drive
Birmingham, AL 35209

To order additional publications, call 1-800-633-4910.

From Liz and Marianne

Each season gives us a gift. Spring offers blossoming fruit trees, bright green tufts of grass, and breezes softly scented with the perfume of blooming flowers. Summer wraps us in all the warmth and the sunshine we could want and provides long hours of outdoor play. Fall bestows swirls of red and gold leaves, a harvest of pumpkins, and an invigorating chill in the air. Winter presents soft blankets of snow and cozy evenings to curl up by the fireplace.

In celebration of these wonderful gifts, we wanted to give you something as well. We have received so many requests from our readers for seasonal quilt patterns that we decided to search through all the issues of *For the Love of Quilting* and compile 28 of the best season-celebrating quilts. So wrapped between the covers of this book is a full year of our favorites.

We feel that every time of year is a wonderful time to quilt, and each season inspires us. The quilts in this book capture the essence of what the seasons have to offer: bright buzzing bees and kites fluttering in the breeze; sailboats bobbing on the horizon and an American flag waving proudly; a big pile of autumn leaves and a happy jack-o'-lantern; a lush poinsettia and fragrant evergreens.

So pour yourself a glass of lemonade or a cup of cocoa—depending upon the season—and flip through these pages. Because no matter what the season of your life, we have a quilt for you.

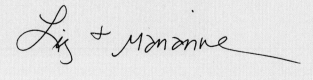

Contents

Page 22

Page 48

Page 60

Page 115

Winter

In the Sewing Room

 **Spring** is one of our favorite times of year to quilt. We often plan a sewing party for early **May.** We gather with friends in Liz's studio with the

patio doors open wide so that we can enjoy the **fresh air.**  As each quilt comes  together, it is as thrilling to see as a new **flower** or the first **robin** in the yard.

Country French Pansies

Liz Porter designed and made this quilt, using Fons & Porter's Country French fabric collection by Benartex, Inc.

Finished Size: 30½" x 30½"   Blocks: 4 (9") Pansy Blocks

materials

⅜ yard white with navy stripe for background

⅛ yard medium gold

⅛ yard light gold

⅛ yard gold-and-blue floral

⅛ yard light blue print

¼ yard medium blue print for sashing

1 yard large gold-and-blue floral for border and binding

1 yard fabric for backing

Craft-size batting

Paper-backed fusible web (optional)

cutting

Measurements include ¼" seam allowance. Patterns are finished size. Add ³⁄₁₆" seam allowance for hand appliqué. Follow manufacturer's instructions if using paper-backed fusible web and trace patterns finished size.

From white with navy stripe, cut:
- 1 (9½"-wide) strip. Cut strip into 4 (9½") background squares.

From medium gold, cut:
- 8 Bs.

From light gold, cut:
- 8 Cs.

From gold-and-blue floral, cut:
- 4 Bs.

From light blue print, cut:
- 4 As.
- 4 A rev.

From medium blue print, cut:
- 4 Ds.
- 3 (2"-wide) strips. Cut strips into 3 (2" x 23") sashing strips and 6 (2" x 9½") sashing strips.

From large gold-and-blue floral, cut:
- 4 (4½"-wide) strips. Cut strips into 2 (4½" x 23") top and bottom borders and 2 (4½" x 31") side borders.
- 4 (2¼"-wide) strips for binding.

block assembly

1. Referring to *Block Diagram*, position pieces in alphabetical order on background square and hand- or machine-appliqué.

2. Make 4 Pansy blocks. ⟶

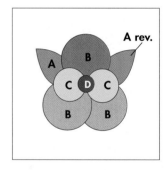

Block Diagram

❀ *I used a machine satin stitch to appliqué the pansies. However, these shapes are easy to handstitch, if you prefer.*
                                                          — *Liz*

quilt assembly

1. Referring to *Quilt Top Assembly Diagram*, alternate 2 Pansy Blocks and 3 (2" x 9½") sashing strips. Join into a block row. Repeat.

2. Alternate block rows with remaining sashing strips. Join to complete center.

3. Add 4½" x 23" borders to top and bottom of quilt top. Press seam allowance toward borders. Add remaining 2 borders to quilt sides.

quilting and finishing

1. Layer backing, batting, and quilt top; baste. Quilt as desired. Quilt shown was machine-quilted in double waves through sashing, following the floral pattern in border. Block backgrounds were filled with echo quilting.

2. Join 2¼"-wide large gold-and-blue floral strips into 1 continuous piece for straight-grain French-fold binding. Add binding to quilt.

Quilt Top Assembly Diagram

Quilt made by Liz Porter

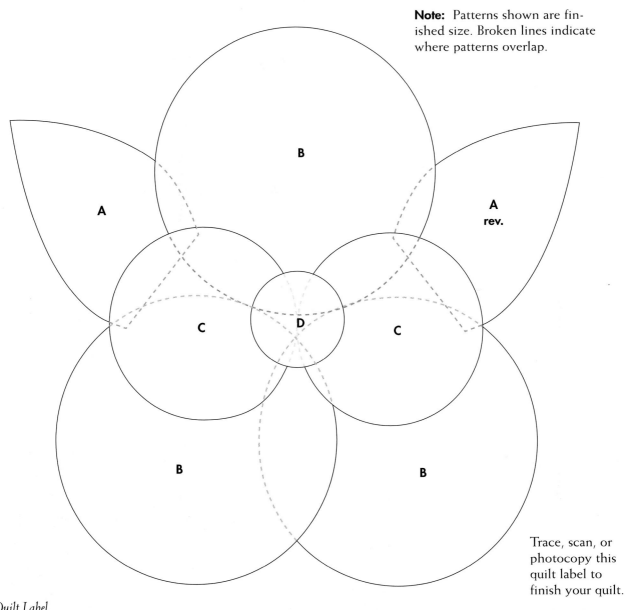

Note: Patterns shown are finished size. Broken lines indicate where patterns overlap.

Trace, scan, or photocopy this quilt label to finish your quilt.

Quilt Label

Floral Trellis

"A confirmed 'fabricaholic'," says Liz Porter, "I began adding 1930s-style prints to my fabric stash as they became plentiful in quilt shops. I pieced this quilt to showcase a small part of my collection."

Finished Size: 82¾" x 101¾"

Blocks: 32 (9") Setting Squares, 49 (4½") Flower Blocks, and 80 (4½" x 9") Leaf Blocks

materials

49 (6½") squares assorted 1930s prints for flower blocks

¼ yard yellow for flower blocks

3 yards green for leaf blocks and binding

7½ yards cream for center, setting triangles, and blocks

⅜ yard pink for piping

10½ yards ⅛"-diameter cording for piping

7½ yards backing

Queen-size batting

cutting

Measurements include ¼" seam allowance.

From assorted 1930s prints, cut:

- 49 sets of:
  - 2 (2" x 5") rectangles (B).
  - 2 (2") squares (C).

From yellow, cut:

- 3 (2"-wide) strips. Cut strips into 49 (2") squares (C).

From green, cut:

- 19 (2½"-wide) strips. Cut strips into 320 (2½") squares (D).
- 20 (1"-wide) strips. Cut strips into 80 (1" x 9½") rectangles (G).
- 10 (2¼"-wide) strips for binding.

From cream, cut:

- 1 (13¾"-wide) strip. Cut strip into 2 (13¾") squares. Cut squares in half diagonally to make 4 corner setting triangles (J).
- 2 (20⅜"-wide) strips. Cut strips into 4 (20⅜") squares. Cut squares into quarters diagonally to make 14 side setting triangles (I). (Two are extra.)
- 8 (9½"-wide) strips. Cut strips into 32 (9½") squares (H).
- 10 (2"-wide) strips. Cut strips into 196 (2") squares (A).
- 19 (2½"-wide) strips. Cut strips into 320 (2½") squares (D).
- 23 (1½"-wide) strips. Cut strips into 640 (1½") squares (E).
- 6 (2½"-wide) strips. Cut strips into 160 (1½" x 2½") rectangles (F).

From pink, cut:

- 10 (1"-wide) strips for piping.

block assembly

1. To make a Flower Block, choose 1 matching set of 2 Bs and 2 Cs. Referring to *Diagonal Seams Diagram 1*, lay 1 A atop 1 end of B. Stitch diagonally as shown. Trim ¼" from stitching and press open. Repeat at other end to complete A/B unit. Repeat to make a second A/B unit.

2. Referring to *Flower Block Assembly Diagram*, join 1 print C to each side of 1 yellow C. Join A/B units to top and bottom to complete block (*Flower Block Diagram*). Make 49 Flower Blocks. ⟶

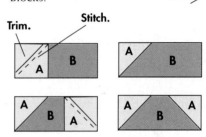

Diagonal Seams Diagram 1

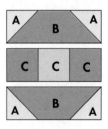

Flower Block Assembly Diagram

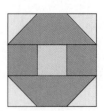

Flower Block Diagram

3. Referring to *Diagonal Seams Diagram 2*, lay 1 E atop 1 corner of green D. Stitch, trim, and press open as before. Repeat on opposite corner. Repeat to make 4 leaf units.

4. Join 4 leaf units, 4 cream Ds, 2 cream Fs, and 1 green G as shown in *Leaf Block Assembly Diagram* to complete block (*Leaf Block Diagram*). Make 80 Leaf Blocks.

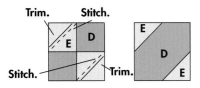

Diagonal Seams Diagram 2

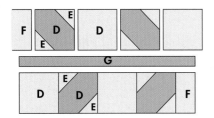

Leaf Block Assembly Diagram

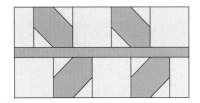

Leaf Block Diagram

quilt assembly

1. Referring to top right corner of *Quilt Top Assembly Diagram*, join 1 Leaf Block to opposite sides of 1 cream block (H). Join 1 Flower Block to opposite ends of 1 Leaf Block. Add to top of block as shown. Add 1 side setting triangle (I) to ends to complete first row.

2. Continue in this manner, carefully following *Quilt Top Assembly Diagram*. Join rows, matching seams; then add corner setting triangles (J) to complete quilt top.

❀ *Use a zipper foot to stitch the binding close to the piping.*
— *Liz*

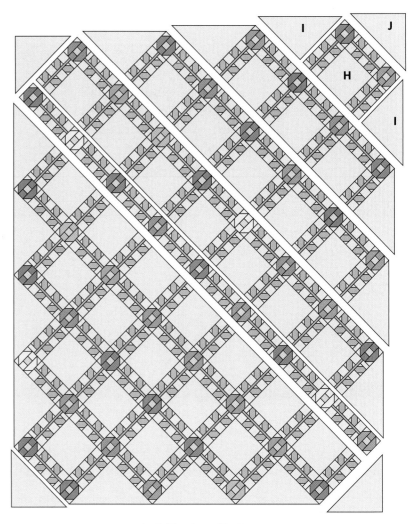

Quilt Top Assembly Diagram

quilting and finishing

1. Divide backing fabric into 3 (2½-yard) lengths. Join along long sides to make backing. Seams will run horizontally.

2. Layer backing, batting, and quilt top; baste. Quilt as desired. Quilt shown has outline quilting in flowers and leaves and a circle in center of each flower. Cream blocks and setting triangles feature a feathered circle design.

3. Join pink strips into 1 continuous piece to make cording cover. Fold in half lengthwise, right sides out, and insert cording. Using zipper foot, baste to secure cording inside piping. With raw edges aligned, baste cording to quilt top.

4. Join 2¼"-wide green strips into 1 continuous piece for straight-grain French-fold binding. Add binding to quilt.

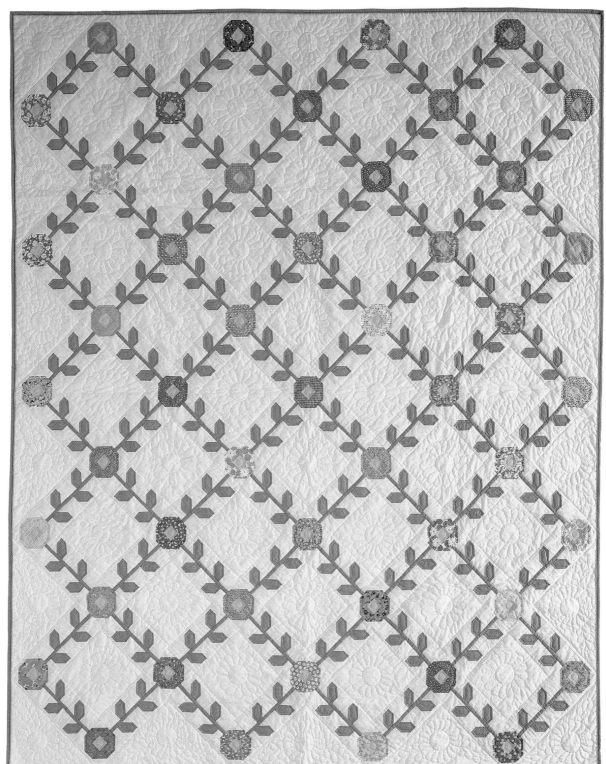

Quilt designed and made by Liz Porter; hand-quilted by Toni Fisher

Spring **15**

Bee Bop

This honey of a quilt makes full use of bright fabrics set against a black background. There's a special surprise on the back: even more bees are buzzing there (see page 20).

Finished Size: 48" x 48"

materials

3 yards black for background and
    binding

¼ yard yellow for bees

⅛ yard black-and-white check for bee
    wings

1¼ yards green (¾ yard for bias vine;
    remaining in assorted shades ⅛- or
    ¼-yard cuts)

⅛ yard or fat eighths* each 2 yellows,
    2 or 3 light oranges, 2 corals,
    2 pinks, 3 or 4 purples, and 3 or
    4 blues

3 yards solid fabric for backing (See
    page 20 for additional materials for
    appliquéd backing.)

54" x 54" scrap batting

Gold metallic embroidery thread

*Fat eighth = 9" x 22"

bee cutting and assembly

(10 bees for front of quilt)

From black, cut:

- 2 (1¾"-wide) strips. Cut strips
  into 30 (1¾") squares for head
  background.
- 1 (3¼"-wide) strip. Cut strip into 10
  (3¼") squares for body background.
- 3 (¾"-wide) strips. Reserve for bee
  body stripes.

From yellow, cut:

- 4 (1¼"-wide) strips. Reserve for bee
  body stripes.
- 10 bee heads, using pattern on page
  21 and adding ¼" seam allowance.

From black/white check, cut:

- 2 (1¾"-wide) strips. Cut strips into
  20 (1¾" x 3¼") rectangles for wings.

1. Join 4 yellow strips and 3 black
strips alternately into a strip set (see
Diagram 1). Using pattern on page 21,

cut 10 bee bodies, adding ¼" seam
allowance.

2. Using diagonal-seams method, join
1 (1¾") black square to 1 black-and-
white rectangle (see *Diagram 2*). Make 10
right wings and 10 left wings as shown.

3. Lay out 1 small black square, 1 large
black square, 1 left wing, and 1 right
wing (see *Diagram 3*). Join into rows; join
rows to complete bee background.

4. Appliqué bee body and bee head in
place, using your favorite appliqué technique (see *Bee Diagram*).

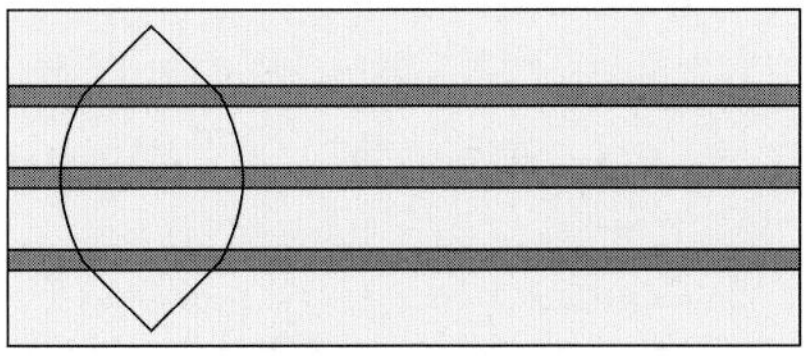

Diagram 1

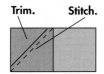

Trim.   Stitch.

Diagram 2

 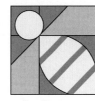

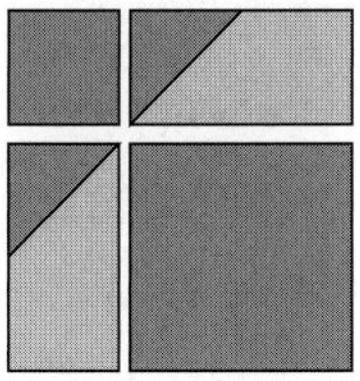

Diagram 3   *Bee Diagram*

center cutting and assembly

From black, cut:

- 1 (2½"-wide) strip. Cut strip into
  16 (2½") squares for center.
- 3 (2⅞"-wide) strips. Cut strips into
  41 (2⅞") squares. Cut squares in half
  diagonally to make 82 half-square
  triangles for center.
- 2 (1½") squares for odd flower block.
- 1 (1⅞") square for odd flower block.

From green, cut:

- 1 (2⅞"-wide) strip. Cut strip into
  7 (2⅞") squares. Cut squares in half
  diagonally to make 14 half-square
  triangles for center.

**From yellows, light oranges, and
    corals, cut from each:**

- 1 (2⅞"-wide) strip. Cut strip into
  2 (2⅞") squares. Cut squares in half
  diagonally to make 4 half-square
  triangles for flower.
- 2 (2½") squares for flower.
- Reserve remainder for Goose Chase
  border.

From pinks, cut:

- 1 (2⅞"-wide) strip. Cut strip into
  2 (2⅞") squares. Cut squares in half
  diagonally to make 4 half-square
  triangles for odd flower.
- 2 (2½") squares for odd flower.
- 3 (2⅞") squares. Cut squares in half
  diagonally to make 6 half-square triangles for center. Reserve remainder
  for Goose Chase border.

From purples, cut:

- 2 (2½") squares for odd flower.
- 1 (2⅞") square. Cut square in half
  diagonally to make 2 half-square
  triangles for odd flower. You will
  have 1 extra.
- 3 (1½") squares for odd flower.
- 1 (1⅞") square for odd flower.
- 14 (2⅞") squares from at least 3 different shades of purple. Cut squares
  in half diagonally to make 28 half-
  square triangles for center. You will
  have 1 extra.

From blues, cut:

- 10 (2⅞") squares from at least
  2 shades of blue. Cut squares in half
  diagonally to make 20 half-square
  triangles for center. ⟶

1. Join 1 black half-square triangle to 1 colored triangle along long edges to make triangle-square. Make 8 pink, 14 green, 20 blue, and 27 purple triangle-squares.

2. Join 1 yellow triangle to 1 black triangle to make triangle-square. Make 4 triangle-squares. Arrange these 4 triangle-squares with 2 yellow squares to make Single Flower Unit (*Single Flower Unit Assembly Diagram*). In same manner, make 1 light orange and 1 coral Single Flower Unit.

3. To make Odd Flower Unit, use diagonal-seams method to join 1 (1½") purple square to 1 corner of 1 (2½") black square. Make 2 black/purple quarter corner units (*Diagram 4*). Repeat,

using 1 (1½") black square and 1 (2½") purple square. Make 2 purple/black quarter corner units.

4. Using 1 green and black triangle-square from Step 1, join 1 (1½") purple square to upper right corner as shown in *Diagram 5*.

5. Join 1 (1⅞") black square to 1 end of 1 purple triangle (*Diagram 6*), aligning point of triangle with side of square. Trim excess. Join 1 pink triangle to complete square. Repeat with 1 black triangle and 1 (1⅞") purple square, joining purple square to opposite end of triangle. Add 1 pink triangle to complete square.

6. Lay out 7 squares from Steps 3–5, along with 1 (2½") black square, 2 (2½") pink squares, and 2 pink-and-black half-square-triangle units (see *Odd Flower Unit Assembly Diagram*).

7. Join into rows; join rows to complete

Odd Flower Block (*Odd Flower Unit Diagram*).

8. Lay out 14 (2½") black squares, 3 bee blocks, 1 odd flower block, 3 single flower units, and 66 color/black half-square-triangle units. Arrange into sections as shown in *Diagram 7*. Rearrange shading and placement of color/black units as desired. Join units into sections; join sections to complete center unit.

borders 1 and 2 cutting and assembly

From black, cut:

- 4 (1½"-wide) strips for Border 1. From these, cut 2 (1½" x 22½") strips for side borders and 2 (1½" x 24½") strips for top and bottom borders.
- For Border 2, cut 2 (4½"-wide) strips. Cut strips into 1 (4½" x 15½") rectangle, 1 (4½" x 10½") rectangle, 3 (4½") squares, 4 (2½" x 4½") rectangles, and 1 (1½" x 4½") rectangle.
- 4 (2½"-wide) strips. Cut strips into 62 (2½") squares for Goose Chase units.

From leftover center colors, cut:

- 31 (2½" x 4½") rectangles, using several shades of each color group: 6 yellow, 6 light orange, 3 coral, 3 pink, 7 purple, and 6 blue.

Refer to *Quilt Top Assembly Diagram* and photo (on page 16) throughout the remainder of instructions.

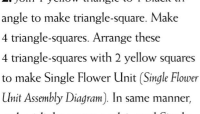

Single Flower Unit Assembly Diagram *Single Flower Unit Diagram*

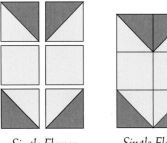

Diagram 4

Diagram 5

Diagram 6

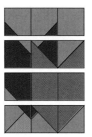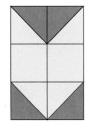

Odd Flower Unit Assembly Diagram *Odd Flower Unit Diagram*

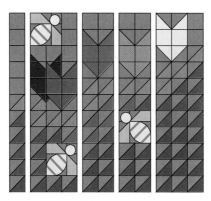

Diagram 7

Goose Chase Diagrams

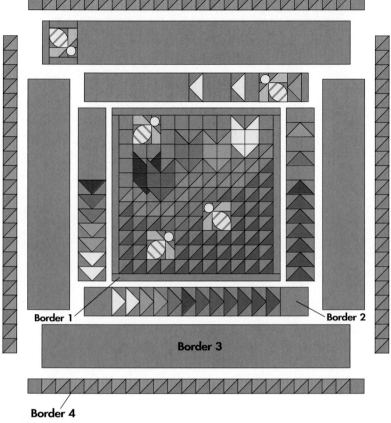

Quilt Top Assembly Diagram

1. For Border 1, join 1 (1½" x 22½") black border to each side of quilt. Join 1 (1½" x 24½") black border to top and bottom of quilt.

2. To make Border 2, using diagonal-seams method, join 1 (2½") black square to each end of 1 (2½" x 4½") color rectangle to make a Goose Chase unit (*Goose Chase Diagrams*). Make 31 Goose Chase units.

3. For left side border, arrange 2 yellow, 2 light orange, and 1 each of coral, pink, and purple Goose Chase units pointing down. Join into strip and add 1 (4½" x 10½") rectangle. Join to left side of quilt center.

4. For right side border, arrange 3 blue, 3 purple, and 1 each of pink, coral, and light orange Goose Chase units pointing up with 3 (2½" x 4½") rectangles as

shown. Join into strip; join to right side of quilt center.

5. For bottom border, arrange 2 yellow, 2 light orange, 1 coral, 1 pink, 3 purple, and 3 blue Goose Chase units pointing right. Add 1 (4½") black square to each end. Join into a strip; add to quilt bottom.

6. For top border, arrange 2 yellow and 1 light orange Goose Chase units, 1 bee block, and remaining 4½"-wide black rectangles as shown. Join into a strip; add to quilt top.

border 3 cutting and assembly

From black, cut:

• 4 (6½"-wide) strips. Cut strips into 2 (6½" x 32½") strips for side borders, 1 (6½" x 39½") strip for top

border, and 1 (6½" x 44½") strip for bottom border (piece if necessary).

• From remainder, cut 1 (1½" x 6½") rectangle and 2 (1½" x 4½") rectangles for bee block sashing.

For appliqué, cut:

• 24 leaves, in at least 3 shades of green, using pattern on page 21.

• 23 tulips in varying shades, using pattern on page 21: 5 light orange, 3 coral, 3 pink, 7 purple, and 5 blue.

• Make approximately 200" of ½"-wide green bias (cut 1½"-wide and then fold and press in thirds) for vine.

1. Join 1 (6½" x 32½") black strip to each side of quilt. Join 1 (6½" x 44½") black strip to bottom edge.

2. Join 1 (1½" x 4½") rectangle to top and bottom of 1 bee block. Join 1 (1½" x 6½") rectangle to left side. Join bee block with sashing to left end of remaining black border. Add to top of quilt.

3. Appliqué vine as shown in photo on page 16. Appliqué leaves and flowers in place.

4. Appliqué 5 remaining bee blocks in place as shown in photo or as desired. With gold metallic thread, stemstitch antennae and stingers for bees and add French knots at ends of antennae.

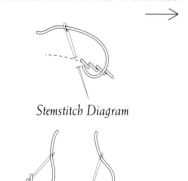

Stemstitch Diagram

French Knot Diagram

border 4 cutting and assembly

From black, cut:

- 4 (2⅞") strips. Cut strips into 44 (2⅞") squares. Cut squares in half diagonally to make 88 half-square triangles.
- 4 (2½") squares.

From assorted greens, cut:

- 4 (2⅞"-wide) strips from at least 2 different shades. Cut strips into 44 (2⅞") squares. Cut squares in half diagonally to make 88 half-square triangles.

1. Join 1 block triangle to 1 green triangle along diagonal. Make 88 triangle-squares.

2. Join 22 triangle units into strip. Make 4 strips.

3. Referring to *Quilt Top Assembly Diagram* on page 19, join 1 strip to each side of quilt, with green toward center.

4. Add 1 (2½") black square to each end of remaining strips. Add to top and bottom of quilt, green toward center, to complete.

quilting and finishing

1. Cut backing into 2 (1½-yard) lengths. Cut 1 piece in half lengthwise. Sew 1 narrow length to 1 side of wide length. Press seam allowances toward narrow length. Remaining narrow length is extra.

2. See "Backing Bees" above to add appliquéd bees to backing.

3. Layer backing, batting, and quilt top; baste. Quilt as desired. Quilt shown was machine-stipple-quilted in all black areas.

4. For binding, cut 5 (2¼"-wide) strips from black fabric. Make approximately 6 yards of French-fold straight-grain binding. Add binding to quilt.

backing bees

materials

⅝ yard black
⅜ yard yellow
¼ yard black-and-white check

cutting

From black, cut:

- 3 (1¾"-wide) strips. Cut strips into 48 (1¾") squares for head background.
- 2 (3¼") strips. Cut strips into 16 (3¼") squares for body background.
- 6 (¾"-wide) strips. Reserve for bee body stripes.

From yellow, cut:

- 8 (1¼"-wide) strips. Reserve for bee body stripes.
- 16 bee heads, using pattern on opposite page and adding ¼" seam allowance.

From black-and-white check, cut:

- 3 (1¾"-wide) strips. Cut strips into 32 (1¾" x 3¼") rectangles for wings.

assembly

Follow Steps 1–4 under Bee Cutting and Assembly on page 17 to make 16 bees. Appliqué at random on back of quilt.

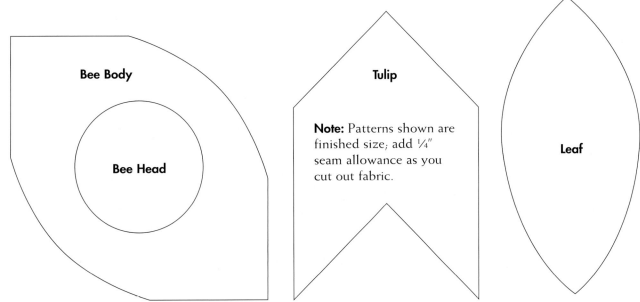

Bee Body

Bee Head

Tulip

Note: Patterns shown are finished size; add ¼" seam allowance as you cut out fabric.

Leaf

Tulip Garden

This charming antique quilt welcomes springtime—and especially Mother's Day—with its colorful blooms. Stitch your own version of this time-honored favorite.

Finished Size: 80" x 80"   Blocks: 16 (16") Tulip Blocks

materials

11 yards white or light muslin for
    background, border, and backing
1¼ yards medium green for stems and F
1½ yards light green for A and B
½ yard dark purple for C and D
½ yard dark gold for C and D
¾ yard purple for E
¾ yard gold for E
¾ yard medium purple for binding
Full-size batting
Template plastic or other material for
    appliqué templates
1 (16½") paper square
Fine-tip permanent marker

cutting

Measurements include ¼" seam allowances. Cut crosswise strips unless otherwise noted. Borders are longer than needed to allow for mitering.

From white or muslin, cut:

- 5 yards for backing.
- 8 (16½"-wide) strips. Cut strips into 16 (16½") squares for block backgrounds.
- 4 (8½"-wide) lengthwise strips for borders. Reserve remaining long piece for hanging sleeve, if needed.

From medium green, cut:

- 4 (9"-wide) strips. Cut strips into 64 (1¼" x 12") bias strips. Fold each

strip in thirds so that each is approximately ⅜" wide; press. Each piece will yield 1 curved stem for a bud and 1 straight stem for a tulip.

- 2 (2¾"-wide) strips. Cut strips into 25 (2¾") squares for F.

From medium purple, cut:

- 8 (2¼"-wide) strips for binding.

Make appliqué templates, using patterns on page 25. Using templates and adding ³⁄₁₆" for seam allowance, cut:

- 32 light green leaves (A).
- 32 light green leaves (A rev.).
- 64 light green leaves (B).
- 32 dark purple tulip buds (C).
- 32 dark gold tulip buds (C).
- 32 dark purple tulip centers (D).
- 32 dark gold tulip centers (D).
- 32 purple tulips (E).
- 32 gold tulips (E).

block assembly

1. Fold background square in half diagonally and crease. Repeat with opposite half. (Crease lines will help in placement of appliqué pieces.)

2. To make a master pattern for appliqué placement, fold 16½" paper square in half horizontally and vertically to make 4 quadrants. Trace tulip pattern (on page 25) in 1 quadrant; fold paper in half and trace in adjacent quadrant. (Second tracing will be a mirror image of first.) Open paper and fold in half to trace into remaining quadrants. Darken traced lines with marker. Position under fabric background square for appliqué placement.

3. Referring to *Half-Block Assembly Diagrams*, gently curve bias strip along placement line in 1 quadrant. Trim stem so that approximately ¼" will extend under C and F. Appliqué curved stem.

→

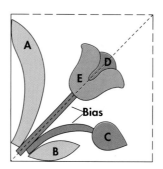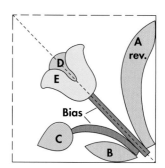

Half-Block Assembly Diagrams

Position and appliqué straight stem so that top edge will be covered by E and bottom by F. Appliqué remaining pieces in alphabetical order as shown. Be sure to leave ¼" seam allowance around block edges. Repeat appliqué in each quadrant, with gold and purple tulips in opposite corners as shown.

4. Make 16 blocks (*Block Diagram*).

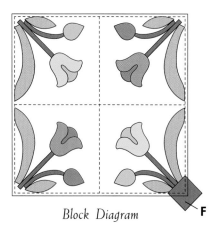

Block Diagram

quilt assembly

1. Referring to photo, lay out blocks into 4 horizontal rows of 4 blocks each. Rotate blocks as shown so that same color tulips "bloom" in clusters. Join blocks in rows; then join rows to complete quilt top.

2. Center and sew 1 border to each side of quilt top. Miter corners and trim excess.

3. Appliqué 1 (2¾") F square over each block corner as shown in photo, turning edges under ¼".

quilting and finishing

1. Divide backing fabric into 2 (2½-yard) lengths. Cut 1 piece in half lengthwise. Sew 1 narrow panel to each side of wide panel. Press seam allowances toward narrow panels.

2. Layer backing, batting, and quilt top; baste. Quilt as desired. Quilt shown was outline-quilted around appliqué motifs and has feathers in the border and in the center of each block. The remaining areas are filled with diagonal quilting.

3. Join 2¼"-wide medium purple strips into 1 continuous piece to make approximately 9½ yards of French-fold straight-grain binding. Add binding to quilt.

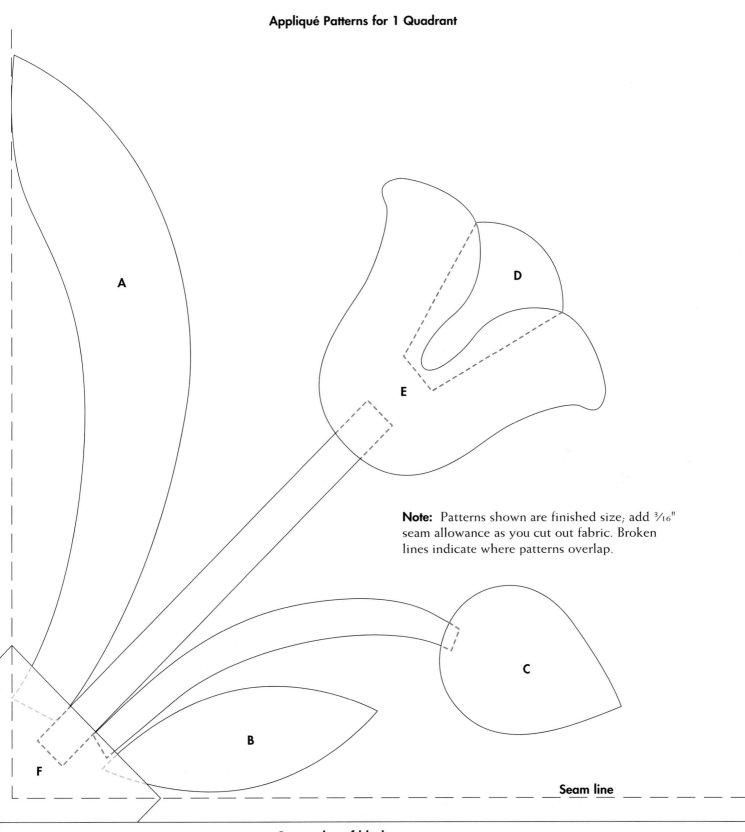

Appliqué Patterns for 1 Quadrant

A

D

E

C

B

F

Note: Patterns shown are finished size; add ³⁄₁₆" seam allowance as you cut out fabric. Broken lines indicate where patterns overlap.

Seam line

Outer edge of block

Chocolate Bunnies

Fusing techniques make quick work of this wall hanging. For added dimension, blanket-stitch around the appliqué shapes or embellish the baskets.

Finished Size: 33" x 42"
Blocks: 6 (9") Double-Nine-Patch Blocks, 6 Appliqué Blocks

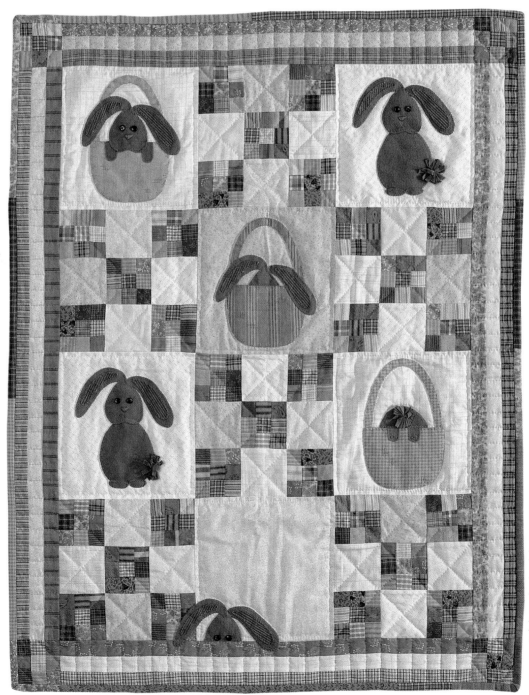

materials

½ yard each 6 assorted light tan prints for background squares, pieced blocks, and middle borders

½ yard each 3 assorted dark tan prints for handles and baskets

¼ yard rose print for inner ear and patchwork

¼ yard brown flannel or brown print for bunnies

¼ yard each of 15 to 20 assorted prints in muted green, rose, and blue for patchwork, borders, and binding

1½ yards green plaid for backing

Crib-size batting

8 small dark brown buttons

½ yard paper-backed fusible web

Rose and brown embroidery floss

cutting

From assorted light tan prints, cut:

- 6 different 9½" background squares.
- 24 (3½") squares for patchwork.
- 2 (1½" x 27½") strips for top and bottom middle borders.
- 2 (1½" x 36½") strips for side middle borders.

From each of 3 dark tan prints, cut:

- 1 handle (J) and 1 basket (K).

From rose print, cut:

- 5 Es and 5 Fs.

From brown flannel, cut:

- 2 As, 5 Bs, 5 Cs, 4 Ds, 2 Gs, 1 H, and 2 Is. Trim bottom of 1 B along red Cutting Line 1. Trim bottom of 1 B along blue Cutting Line 2.

From assorted muted prints, cut:

- 4 (1½" x 27½") strips for top and bottom borders.
- 4 (1½" x 36½") strips for side borders.
- 18 (1½"-wide) strips for patchwork.

From fusible web:

- Trace appliqué patterns on pages 28 and 29 onto paper side of fusible web. Cut out shapes roughly and fuse to wrong side of tan, rose, and brown fabrics, following manufacturer's instructions. Then cut the following:

double-nine-patch block assembly

1. Referring to *Diagram 1*, make 6 strip sets of 3 (1½"-wide) strips each at random. (You may want to use shorter strips for more variety and to use up scraps.) Cut strip sets into 102 (1½"-wide) segments. Join 3 segments each at random to make 34 (3½") Nine-Patch Blocks.

2. Referring to *Diagram 2*, join 5 Nine-Patch Blocks and 4 (3½") light tan squares each to make 6 Double Nine-Patch Blocks. Set aside remaining 4 Nine-Patch Blocks for borders. ⟶

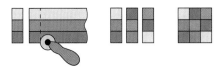

Diagram 1

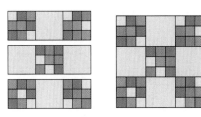

Diagram 2

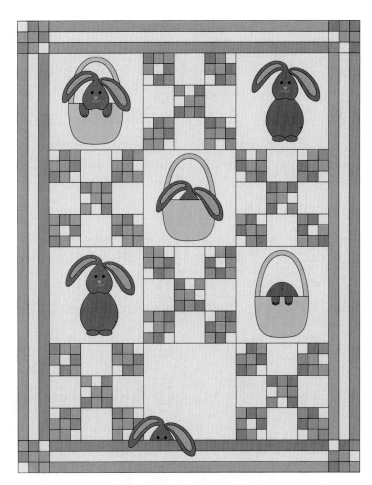

Quilt Top Assembly Diagram

appliqué block assembly

1. Set aside 1 (9½") background square for bottom row. Appliqué for this block will be done after the borders have been added to quilt top.

2. Remove paper backing from all appliqué pieces. Position a handle (J) and basket (K) on each of 3 (9½") light tan squares. Fuse, following manufacturer's instructions.

3. Referring to photo on page 26, position bunny parts on 5 background blocks. Fuse in place.

4. Blanket-stitch around each fused piece with matching floss (see *Blanket-Stitch Diagram*). Embroider nose, mouth, paw pads, and basket details as desired. Add buttons for eyes.

Blanket-Stitch Diagram

Note: B, C, E, and F are reversed for fusing technique.

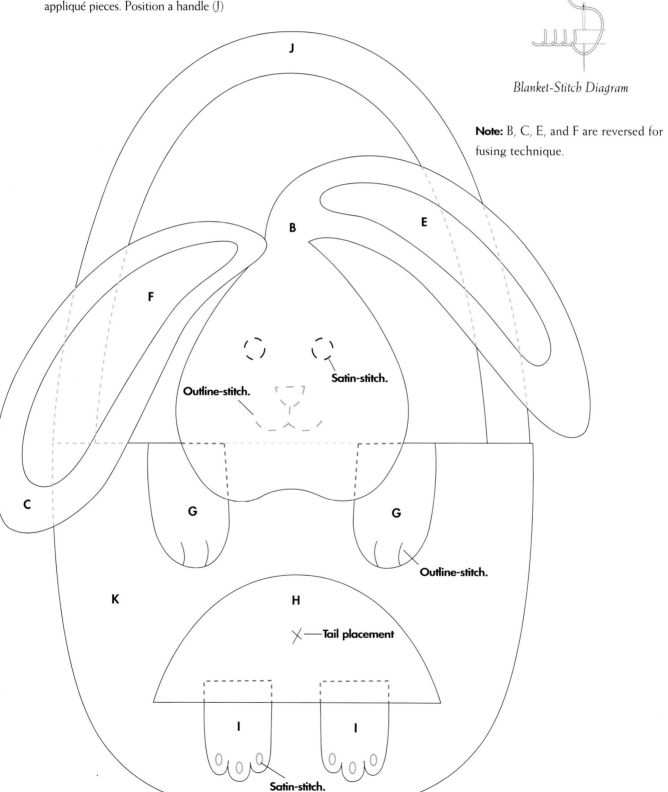

J

B   E

F

Satin-stitch.

Outline-stitch.

C   G   G

Outline-stitch.

K   H

X—Tail placement

I   I

Satin-stitch.

quilt assembly

1. Referring to *Quilt Top Assembly Diagram* on page 27, arrange blocks as shown in 4 horizontal rows of 3 blocks each, adding plain appliqué background block at bottom center. Join into rows; join rows to complete top.

2. Join 3 (1½" x 36½") side border strips along long sides, placing light strip in middle. Repeat for second border strip. Add to each side of quilt top.

3. Join 3 (1½" x 27½") top and bottom border strips along long sides, placing light strip in middle. Repeat for second border strip. Join 1 Nine-Patch Block to each end as shown. Add to top and bottom of quilt, matching seams.

4. Position remaining bunny B, C, E, and F pieces in bottom center block so that ears overlap into left block and bottom border. Fuse in place, embroider, and add buttons.

quilting and finishing

1. Layer backing, batting, and quilt top; baste. Quilt as desired. Quilt has outline-quilting around appliqué and just inside block edges. Double-Nine-Patch Blocks have X through each small block, and border is quilted into 1" sections. Each border corner has square set on point.

2. From brown flannel, cut 1 (¼" x 45") strip for each tail. Loop each strip around 3 fingers and tie in the center with matching embroidery floss. Cut loops open. Thread floss ends into large-eyed needle. Stitch tails in place. Bring ends to back of quilt and tie securely.

3. For binding, cut 3"-wide strips of varying lengths from assorted prints. Make approximately 4½ yards of French-fold straight-grain binding. Add binding to quilt.

Note: B, C, E, and F are reversed for fusing technique.

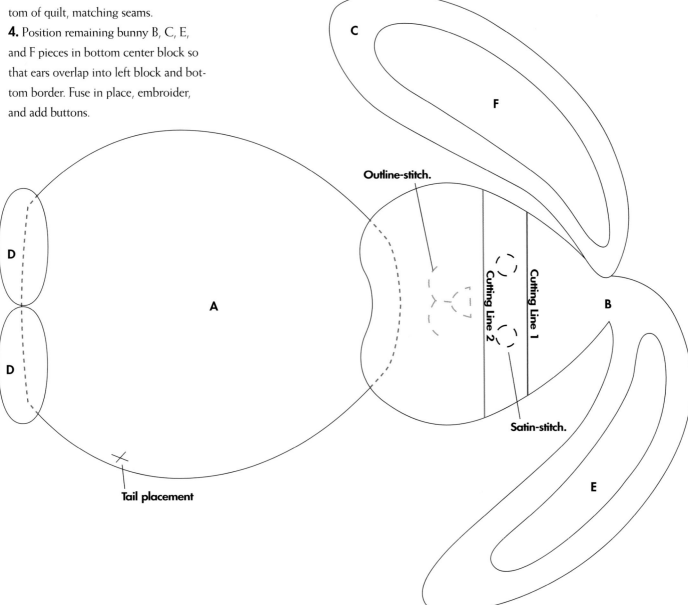

Let's Fly a Kite

Do the lengthening days and warm breezes of March make you long to do something fun? Then go fly a kite—or better still, make Liz's bright and cheerful kite quilt.

Finished Size: 39" x 54"   Blocks: 13 (6" x 15") Kite Blocks, 2 partial blocks

materials

2¼ yards light blue print

Fat eighth* each of 16 bright fabrics for kites, tails, and pieced border

½ yard purple print for binding

1¾ yards fabric for backing

Crib-size quilt batting

13 (9") pieces ⅛"-wide ribbon for tails in colors to coordinate with kites

Clear monofilament nylon thread

*Fat eighth = 9" x 22"

cutting

Before cutting pieces, read instructions carefully. Take extra care when cutting L and R pieces. Measurements include ¼" seam allowances. Cut crosswise strips.

From light blue print, cut:

• 4 (2"-wide) border strips.

• 2 (3⅞"-wide) strips. Cut strips into 15 (3⅞") squares. Cut squares in half diagonally to make 30 A triangles.

• 3 (2¾"-wide) strips. Cut strips into 13 (2¾") squares. Cut squares in quarters diagonally to make 52 B triangles. From remaining strips, cut 26 (2" x 2¾") C rectangles.

• 2 (2"-wide) strips. Cut strips into 13 (1½" x 2") D rectangles and 13 (2" x 4") E rectangles.

• 2 (6½"-wide) strips. Cut strips into 39 (1½" x 6½") F rectangles and 2 (6½") G squares.

• 4 (4¼"-wide) strips. Cut strips into 29 (4¼") squares. Cut squares in quarters diagonally to make 116 H triangles.

• 4 (3⅝"-wide) strips. Cut strips into 16 (3⅝" x 7⅞") rectangles. Referring to *Rectangle Cutting Diagrams*, cut 8 rectangles in half diagonally, from lower right to upper left, to make 16 L triangles for left side of kites. Cut 8 rectangles in half diagonally, from lower left to upper right, to make 16 R triangles for right side of kites. You will have 1 extra of each type piece.

From each bright fabric, cut:

• 1 (3⅝" x 7⅞") rectangle. Referring to *Rectangle Cutting Diagrams*, cut 8 rectangles to make 16 L pieces for left side of kites and 8 rectangles to make 16 R pieces for right side of kites.

• 1 (3⅞") square. Cut square in half diagonally to make 2 A triangles. (You will need a total of 30 for top of kites.)

• 1 (2¾") square. Cut square in quarters diagonally to make 4 B triangles. You will need a total of 52 for kite tails.

• 2 (4¼") squares. Cut squares in quarters diagonally to make 8 H triangles. You will need a total of 116 for borders.

From purple print, cut:

• 5 (2¼"-wide) strips.

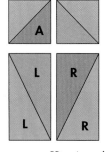
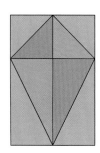

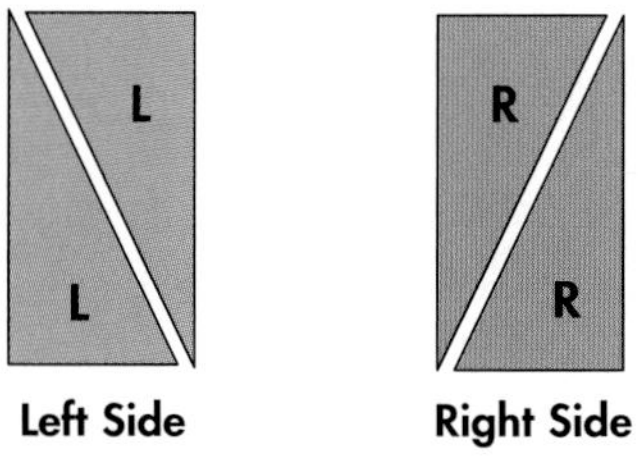

Left Side   Right Side

Rectangle Cutting Diagrams

Kite Assembly Diagrams

block assembly

1. For each kite, select 1 L and 1 A in same color; 1 R and 1 A in contrasting color; and 2 As, 1 L, and 1 R in blue. Referring to *Kite Assembly Diagrams*, join pieces to make 1 kite. (See box on page 32 for tips on joining pieces.) Repeat to make 15 kites.

$\longrightarrow$

joining half-rectangle triangles

When joining R and L units, don't match ends (*Photo A*) as for half-square triangles. If you do, your points will not meet at block corners when you press unit open (*Photo B*). One point will be too far from edge, and other will extend beyond unit.

Instead, offset pieces so that edges intersect and form notch ¼" from side to be seamed, as shown in *Photo C*. When you press unit open, points will meet in corners (*Photo D*). You may want to trim "dog ears" that extend beyond unit.

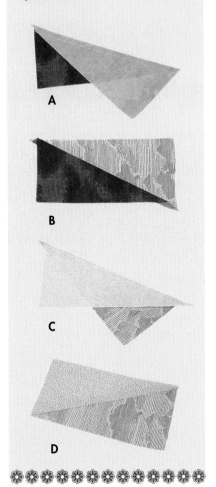

A

B

C

D

2. To make 1 tail unit, choose 4 B tail triangles to match 1 of kite fabrics. Referring to *Quarter-Square Assembly Diagrams*, join bright B triangles to 4 light blue B triangles to make 2 matching units. In this manner, make 2 quarter-square units for each of 13 kite blocks.

3. Referring to *Tail Assembly Diagrams*, lay out 2 quarter-square units, 2 Cs, 1 D, 1 E, and 3 Fs for each tail. Join pieces in rows; then join rows. Make 7 tail units with tail trailing to left and 6 tail units with tail trailing to right by reversing position of D and E rectangles (*Quilt Top Assembly Diagram*).

Quarter-Square Assembly Diagrams

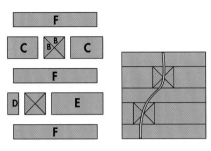

Tail Assembly Diagrams

4. Position 1 piece of ribbon on top of each tail section so that ribbon flows from center top raw edge of section through centers of quarter-square units

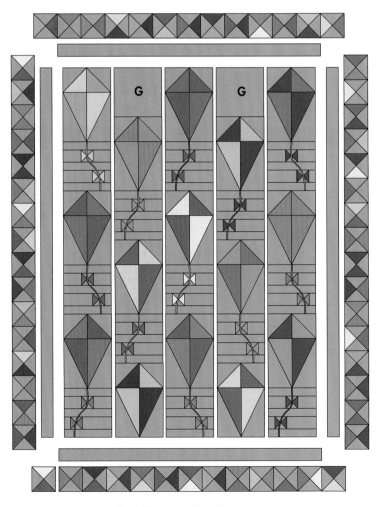

Quilt Top Assembly Diagram

to bottom raw edge. Using mono-filament thread, zigzag ribbon in place. Repeat for all tail sections.

5. Join completed tail units to matching kite units. You will have 13 blocks with tails and 2 kites with no tails for bottom edge of quilt.

quilt assembly

1. Referring to *Quilt Top Assembly Diagram*, lay out kite blocks, partial kite blocks, and G squares. Join pieces in vertical rows; then join rows.

2. Trim 2 (2"-wide) blue borders to 33½" long. Join leftover pieces to remaining strips to make 2 (45½"-long) borders. Join longer borders to quilt sides; then add shorter borders to top and bottom edges. Press seam allowances toward borders.

3. To make pieced border, refer to *Quarter-Square Assembly Diagrams* and join 2 light blue H triangles and 2 different bright H triangles to form square. Repeat to make 58 squares.

4. Referring to *Quilt Top Assembly Diagram* and to photo, make 2 side border units by joining 16 squares for each, turning blocks as shown. Sew borders to quilt sides. In similar manner, join 13 squares each for top and for bottom borders. Sew borders to top and bottom edges of quilt.

quilting and finishing

1. Layer quilt back, batting, and quilt top; baste.

2. Quilt as desired. Quilt shown is outline-quilted in-the-ditch around brightly colored patchwork pieces. Quilted wavy lines across light blue areas resemble wind blowing.

3. Make approximately 200" of French-fold binding and add to quilt. Attach hanging sleeve along top edge of quilt, if desired.

Quilt designed and made by Liz Porter; machine-quilted by Fern Stewart

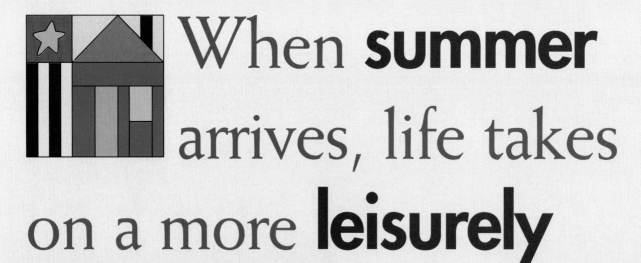 When **summer** arrives, life takes on a more **leisurely** pace. These **lazy** dog days are wonderful times to

plan our next quilts. We may assemble a

small wall hanging kit to work on

while **vacationing.** Or we may select fabrics 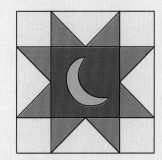 for a quilt that pays tribute to **summertime** activities.

Regatta

Many old quilts have rows and rows of symmetrical patchwork blocks—and then suddenly there's an odd one. We call these "maverick" blocks. This nautical quilt features a humorous maverick block (the capsized boat, second row from the bottom) that seems to shout, "Nobody's perfect!"

Finished Size: 58" x 91"   Blocks: 25 (6" x 8") Boat Blocks

materials

2¼ yards blue-and-white print for block background

⅛ yard red print with white stars for flags

¾ yard white-and-cream print for sails

½ yard total assorted red prints for hulls

¾ yard blue-and-white wave print for sashing

1 yard red-and-white stripe for inner border and binding

2¾ yards blue print for outer border

5½ yards fabric for backing

Full-size batting

cutting

Measurements include ¼" seam allowance. Border strips are cut longer than needed to allow for mitered corners. Cut crosswise strips unless otherwise noted.

From blue-and-white print, cut:

- 3 (2"-wide) strips. Cut strips into 50 (2") squares (B).
- 8 (1"-wide) strips. Cut strips into 48 (1" x 6½") strips (C).
- 3 (3¾"-wide) strips. Cut strips into 12 (3¾" x 7⅜") rectangles. With right sides up, cut rectangles in half diagonally, from lower right to upper left, to make 24 D triangles.
- 2 (3¼"-wide) strips. Cut strips into 12 (3¼" x 6⅜") rectangles. With right sides up, cut rectangles in half diagonally, from lower left to upper right, to make 24 E triangles.
- 2 (1¾"-wide) strips. Cut strips into 12 (1¾" x 3¼") rectangles. With right sides up, cut rectangles in half diagonally, from lower right to upper left, to make 24 F triangles. From remainder, cut 24 (1" x 1½") rectangles (G).
- 3 (8½"-wide) strips. Cut strips into 22 (2½" x 8½") rectangles, 5 (6½" x 8½") rectangles, and 4 (1½" x 8½") rectangles for row spacers. From remainder, cut 1 (6½" x 7") rectangle (H).
- 1 (3½" x 38½") top sashing strip.

From red print with white stars, cut:

- 2 (1¾"-wide) strips. Cut strips into 12 (1¾" x 3¼") rectangles. With right sides up, cut rectangles in half diagonally, from lower right to upper left, to make 24 F triangles.

From white-and-cream print, cut:

- 3 (3¾"-wide) strips. Cut strips into 12 (3¾" x 7⅜") rectangles. With right sides up, cut rectangles in half diagonally, from lower right to upper left, to make 24 D triangles.
- 2 (3¼"-wide) strips. Cut strips into 12 (3¼" x 6⅜") rectangles. With right sides up, cut rectangles in half diagonally, from lower left to upper right, to make 24 E triangles.

From assorted red prints, cut:

- 25 (2" x 6½") rectangles (A).

From blue-and-white wave print, cut:

- 5 (3½" x 38½") sashing strips.
- 1 (5½" x 38½") bottom sashing strip.

From red-and-white stripe, cut:

- 6 (1½"-wide) strips. Reserve 2 strips for top and bottom inner borders. Join 2 strips, matching stripes, to make 1 inner side border. Repeat for second side border.
- 8 (2¼"-wide) strips for binding.

From blue print, cut:

- 4 (9½"-wide) lengthwise strips for outer border.   ⟶

✦ *Joining half-rectangle triangles is tricky. To offset the pieces correctly before sewing, you may find it helpful to mark a ¼" seam line on the first few pieces you join. Then read the tip box on page 39 carefully.*
— Liz

block assembly

Refer to *Block Assembly Diagram* throughout.

1. Place 1 B atop 1 end of A. Using diagonal-seams method, stitch diagonally as shown in *Hull Assembly Diagrams*. Trim excess and open. Repeat for other end. Add 1 C to top to make hull unit.

2. Join 1 blue D and 1 white D to make right sail unit, as shown in *Sail Assembly Diagrams*.

3. Join 1 blue E and 1 white E to make left sail unit. Join 1 blue F and 1 red F to make flag unit.

4. Join 1 blue G to end of flag unit. Add to top of E sail unit. Join 1 C to right side of E sail unit.

5. Join units to complete Boat Block. Make 24 Boat Blocks (*Boat Block Diagram*).

6. To make Overturned Boat Block, join 1 B to each end of 1 A. Join to H to complete block as shown in *Overturned Boat Block Diagram.*

quilt assembly

1. Five of the horizontal boat rows have 4 boat blocks, 1 (6½"-wide) spacer, and 4 (2½"-wide) spacers. The Overturned Boat row has 4 Boat Blocks, 1 Overturned Boat Block, 2 (2½"-wide) spacers, and 4 (1½"-wide) spacers. Lay out blocks and join into rows as shown.

2. Alternate 3½"-wide sashing strips and block rows as shown. Add 5½"-wide sashing strip to quilt bottom.

3. Fold red-and-white stripe borders in half to find centers and mark with pins.

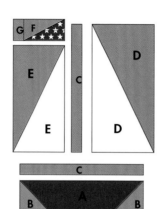

Block Assembly Diagram

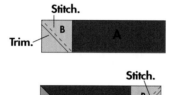

Hull Assembly Diagrams

Repeat for blue borders. Matching center pins, join each red-and-white stripe border to a blue border. Press seam allowance toward blue border.

4. Center borders on all quilt sides. Add to quilt top, mitering corners.

quilting and finishing

1. Divide backing fabric into 2 (2¾-yard) lengths. Cut 1 length into a 25"-wide panel. Sew 25"-wide panel to 1 side of wide panel. Press seam allowance toward narrow panel. Remaining narrow panel is extra.

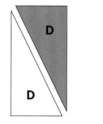

Sail Assembly Diagrams

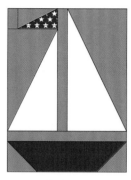

Boat Block Diagram

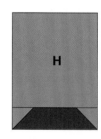

Overturned Boat Block Diagram

2. Layer backing, batting, and quilt top; baste. Quilt as desired. Quilt shown was outline-quilted around boat pieces. Background and sashing were quilted in a wave pattern. Outer border features a rope pattern.

3. Join 2¼"-wide red-and-white stripe strips into 1 continuous piece for straight-grain French-fold binding, matching stripes. Add binding to quilt.

Quilt Top Assembly Diagram

Quilt made by Mary Hickey

working with half-rectangle triangles

If you're used to working with half-square triangles, you may not be used to what happens to the ¼″ seam allowance in half-rectangle triangles. If you follow the directions below, your blocks will come out correctly.

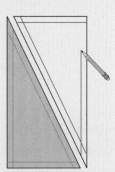

Diagram 1

1. In order to see what happens to ¼″ seam allowance, take your ruler and draw sewing line ¼″ all around wrong side of half-rectangle pieces as shown in *Diagram 1.*

2. See how far the point of fabric extends beyond the sewing line you just drew? It is longer than ¼″. You cannot just align raw edges when you join 2 triangles together; seam lines would not be aligned. Rather, you must pin-match 2 pieces at ¼″ seam line intersection, which looks like elongated X (circled in red in *Diagram 2*) before sititching them together.

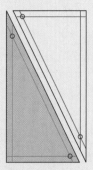

Diagram 2

3. If you have sewn pieces together accurately, drawn lines should match, and you should have tail at each end, as shown in *Diagram 3.*

Diagram 3

4. Trim excess tail and seam allowance even with sides of rectangle unit. At this stage, diagonal seam will not split unit exactly in half *(Diagram 4)*. Don't worry: This is how it should look. When rectangle units are joined to other pieces with ¼″ seams, diagonal split will be at corners.

Diagram 4

Around the Twist

Snowball Blocks are easy to make with the diagonal-seams method. Combine them with Twist Blocks for a straight-seam quilt with the illusion of curves.

Finished Size: 55" x 67"   Blocks: 40 (6") Snowball Blocks, 40 (6") Twist Blocks

materials

½ yard red sunflower print for blocks

½ yard small red print for blocks

1½ yards medium green print for blocks

½ yard green grid print for blocks

1 yard light yellow print for blocks

¼ yard medium yellow print for pieced inner border (1¾ yards for unpieced borders)

1¼ yards dark red print for pieced outer border and binding (2 yards for unpieced borders)

4 yards red print for backing

Twin-size batting

cutting

Measurements include ¼" seam allowances. Cut crosswise strips. Border strips are exact length needed. You may want to cut them longer to allow for piecing variations.

From red sunflower print, cut:

• 5 (2"-wide) strips. Cut strips into 40 (2" x 5") rectangles.

• 2 (2"-wide) strips. Cut strips into 40 (2") squares for diagonal corners.

From small red print, cut:

• 5 (2"-wide) strips. Cut strips into 40 (2" x 5") rectangles.

• 2 (2"-wide) strips. Cut strips into 40 (2") squares for diagonal corners.

From medium green print, cut:

• 7 (6½"-wide) strips. Cut strips into 40 (6½") squares for Snowball Blocks.

From green grid print, cut:

• 4 (3½"-wide) strips. Cut strips into 40 (3½") squares for Twist Blocks.

From light yellow print, cut:

• 10 (2"-wide) strips. Cut strips into 80 (2" x 5") rectangles.

• 4 (2"-wide) strips. Cut strips into 80 (2") squares for Snowball Blocks.

From medium yellow print, cut:

• 7 (1"-wide) strips. Piece strips end to end to make 2 (1" x 48½") top and bottom borders and 2 (1" x 61½") side borders. If you prefer unpieced borders, cut 4 (1"-wide) lengthwise strips to border lengths specified.

From dark red print, cut:

• 7 (3½"-wide) strips. Piece strips end to end to make 2 (3½" x 49½") top and bottom borders and 2 (3½" x 67½") side borders. For unpieced borders, cut 4 (3½"-wide) lengthwise strips to border lengths specified.

• 7 (2¼"-wide) strips for straight-grain binding.

snowball block assembly

1. Using diagonal-seams method, lay 1 (2") yellow print square on 1 (6½") medium green square, right sides facing, aligning corners as shown in *Diagram 1*. Sew across diagonal of small square. Trim excess fabric to ¼" from seam.

Open out yellow triangle. Repeat in each corner.

2. Make 20 blocks with yellow corners.

3. Using diagonal-seams method, stitch 2 (2") small red print squares and 2 (2") red sunflower print squares in alternate corners of 1 (6½") medium green square (*Diagram 2*). Trim excess.

4. Make 20 blocks with red corners. ———→

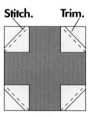

Diagram 1

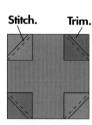

Diagram 2

twist block assembly

1. Align right end of 2" x 5" small red print rectangle to top right corner of 3½" green grid print square. Stitch from top right corner of green square, leaving last 1" of seam unsewn (*Diagram 3*).

2. Add 1 (2" x 5") light yellow print rectangle to right side of unit. Continue with 1 (2" x 5") red sunflower print rectangle on bottom and 1 (2" x 5") light yellow print rectangle on left side. Finish first partial seam by stitching top red strip to remaining portion of green square and yellow strip (*Diagram 4*).

3. Make 40 Twist Blocks.

Diagram 3

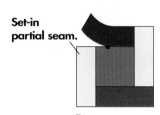

Set-in partial seam.

Diagram 4

quilt assembly

1. To make Row A, lay out 4 Twist Blocks and 4 Snowball Blocks with red corners, orienting as shown in *Quilt Top Assembly Diagram*. Join into row. Make 3 Row As.

2. To make Row B, lay out 4 Twist Blocks and 4 Snowball Blocks with yellow corners, orienting as shown. Join into row. Make 3 Row Bs.

3. To make Row C, lay out 4 Twist Blocks and 4 Snowball Blocks with red corners, orienting as shown. Join into row. Make 2 Row Cs.

4. To make Row D, lay out 4 Twist

Blocks and 4 Snowball Blocks with yellow corners, orienting as shown. Join into row. Make 2 Row Ds.

5. Referring to *Quilt Top Assembly Diagram*, join rows as shown.

6. Join 1 (1" x 48½") medium yellow border to top and bottom of quilt. Join 1 (1" x 61½") border to quilt sides.

7. Join 1 (3½" x 49½") dark red border to top and bottom of quilt. Join 1 (3½" x 67½") border to quilt sides.

quilting and finishing

1. Divide backing fabric into 2 (2-yard) lengths. Cut 1 piece in half lengthwise.

Sew 1 narrow panel to 1 side of wide panel. Press seam allowances toward narrow panel. Remaining narrow panel is extra.

2. Layer backing, batting, and quilt top; baste. Quilt as desired. Quilt shown was outline-quilted ¼" inside red strips and has a single heart inside each green square. The medium green octagonal pieces have a heart pattern.

3. Make approximately 7 yards of French-fold straight-grain binding. Add binding to quilt.

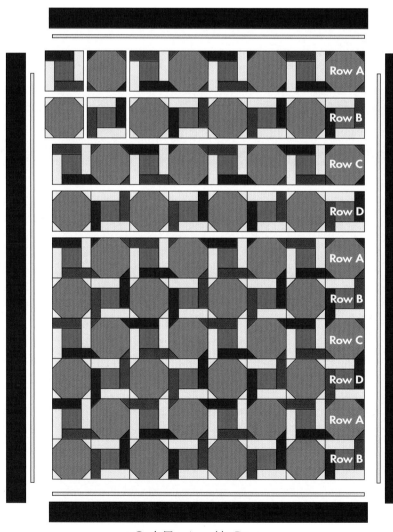

Quilt Top Assembly Diagram

Quilt designed and made by Karen Combs; quilted by Lolita Rawlins

Courthouse Square Wall Quilt

Iowa quilter Marty Freed used mostly plaids and stripes for this homey nine-block quilt. Quick cutting of the blocks, buttonhole-stitch appliquéing, and utility quilting all add up to a charming, fast project.

Finished Size: 44" x 44"   Blocks: 5 (12") Courthouse Square Blocks, 4 (12") Star Blocks

materials

⅛ yard each or scraps of 5 red plaids for flag sections and chimneys

⅛ yard each or scraps of 5 light plaid or print fabrics for flag sections

Scraps at least 4½" square of 5 blue plaid fabrics for flag tops

⅛ yard each or scraps of 5 dark plaid fabrics for Courthouse Square Blocks

⅛ yard total of assorted light, medium, and dark plaids for doors, house peaks, and skies

⅛ yard total of assorted gold fabric scraps for stars, windows, and moons

Scraps at least 6½" square of 4 dark plaids for Star Block centers

⅛ yard each or scraps of 4 light plaids or prints for background of Star Blocks

Scraps at least 3½" square in various dark plaids for Star points (Marty used 8 different fabrics for each of 4 blocks, making 1 block each with red, green, purple, and blue points.)

¼ yard light red plaid for inner border

⅛ yard dark red plaid for unfilled piping border

⅝ yard dark blue stripe for outer border

½ yard dark blue plaid for binding

2⅔ yards fabric for backing

48" x 48" piece of batting

Rotary cutter, acrylic ruler, and cutting mat

Optional: paper-backed fusible web or template material, embroidery floss, and needle

cutting

Measurements for cutting include ¼" seam allowance. Cut all strips crosswise. Make templates for moon and star appliqué patterns (on page 47) or trace moon pattern 4 times and star pattern 5 times onto paper side of fusible web. Follow manufacturer's instructions to fuse to fabrics.

For Courthouse Square Blocks

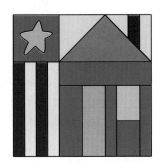

From each red plaid, cut:
- 2 (1½" x 8½") rectangles for flag sections.
- 1 (1½" x 4½") rectangle for chimney.

From each light plaid or print, cut:
- 2 (1½" x 8½") rectangles for flag sections.

From blue plaids, cut:
- 5 (4½") squares for flag tops.

From dark plaids for Courthouse Square Blocks, cut:
- 5 sets of matching pieces for houses: 2 (1½" x 6½") rectangles, 1 (2½" x 6½") rectangle, 1 (2½" x 3½") rectangle, and 1 (2½" x 8½") rectangle.

From scraps of various plaids and prints, cut:
- 5 (2½" x 6½") rectangles for doors.
- 5 (2½" x 3½") rectangles for windows from tan or gold.
- 5 (4½" x 8½") rectangles for house peaks.
- 5 sets of matching pieces for sky: 1 (4½") square, 1 (2½" x 4½") rectangle, and 1 (1½" x 4½") rectangle.
- 4 stars for appliqué.

For Star Blocks

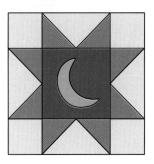

From each dark plaid for Star centers, cut:
- 1 (6½") square.

From light plaids or prints for backgrounds of each Star Block, cut:
- 4 (3½") squares.
- 1 (7 1/4") square. Cut square in quarters diagonally to make 4 triangles.

From scraps for Star points, for each block, cut:
- 8 (3⅞") squares. Cut each square in half diagonally to make 2 triangles. You will have 1 extra.

From leftover gold plaid fabric scraps, for each block, cut:
- 1 moon for appliqué.

For Borders

From light red plaid, cut:
- 4 (1½"-wide) inner border strips.

From dark red plaid, cut:
- 4 (¾"-wide) piping border strips.

From dark blue stripe, cut:
- 5 (3½"-wide) outer border strips. ⟶

assembly
Making Courthouse Square Blocks

1. Referring to *Courthouse Square Block Assembly Diagram*, join 2 each 1½" x 8½" red plaid and light print strips to make lower flag section. Press seam allowances toward red strips. Join 4½" blue plaid square to 1 end to complete flag section. Press seam allowances toward square.

2. Join 2½" x 3½" house rectangle to 1 short side of window rectangle to make window unit.

3. Join 1 (2½" x 6½") house rectangle, 1 door rectangle, 1 (1½" x 6½") house rectangle, 1 window unit, and 1 (1½" x 6½") house rectangle into a row as shown. Press seam allowances toward darker fabrics. Add 2½" x 8½" rectangle to top of row.

4. Join 1 (2½" x 4½") sky rectangle, 1 chimney rectangle, and 1 (1½" x 4½") sky rectangle to form chimney/sky unit. Press seam allowances toward chimney.

5. Using diagonal-seams method, position chimney/sky square, right sides facing, atop right end of house peak rectangle and stitch as shown in *Diagonal Seams Diagram 1*. Trim excess chimney/sky unit as shown in *Diagonal Seams Diagram 2*. Open out chimney/sky triangle and press as shown in *Diagonal Seams Diagram 3*.

6. Referring to *Diagonal Seams Diagrams 4* and *5*, use diagonal-seams method to stitch 4½" sky square to left end of house peak triangle. Trim and press.

7. Sew house peak unit to top of house section. Add flag section to left side of house.

8. Hand- or machine-appliqué star to flag square (see opposite page for *Blanket-Stitch Diagram*). If using fusible

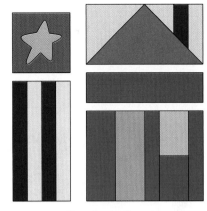

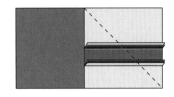

Courthouse Square Block Assembly Diagram

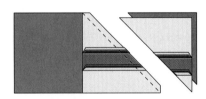

Diagonal Seams Diagram 1

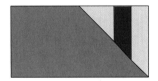

Diagonal Seams Diagram 2

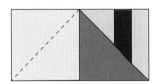

Diagonal Seams Diagram 3

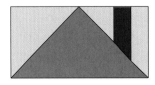

Diagonal Seams Diagram 4

Diagonal Seams Diagram 5

web, follow manufacturer's instructions.

9. Repeat to make a total of 5 Courthouse Square Blocks.

Making Star Blocks

1. Referring to *Side Unit Diagram*, join matching triangles to large light triangles to make 4 side units.

2. Referring to *Star Block Assembly Diagram*, join side units and squares to make rows. Press seam allowances toward squares. Join rows.

3. Hand- or machine-appliqué moon to center square.

4. Repeat to make a total of 4 Star Blocks.

Side Unit Diagram

Star Block Assembly Diagram

assembling quilt top

1. Join blocks in 3 rows of 3 blocks each, as shown in *Quilt Top Assembly Diagram*; then join rows.

2. Measure width of quilt top. Trim 2 light red plaid borders to this measurement. Join to top and bottom edges of quilt top. Measure length of quilt top. Trim 2 remaining red plaid borders to this measurement. Join borders to sides of quilt top.

3. To make unfilled piping, fold and press dark red plaid strips in half lengthwise, wrong sides facing. Measure quilt and trim piping to 4 equal pieces. Pin or baste piping to quilt edges, aligning raw edges of piping with raw edges of red plaid border.

4. Measure width of quilt and trim 2 blue stripe border strips to this measurement. Lay blue stripe border atop top piping border. Join to quilt top, stitching through all layers. Press seam allowances toward dark blue border. Repeat for bottom of quilt top. Measure quilt and trim remaining borders to size. Add to sides of quilt top. (You may need to piece strips to achieve necessary length.)

quilting and finishing

1. Mark desired quilting designs on quilt top.

2. Divide backing fabric into 2 (48"-long) lengths. Cut 1 (6" x 48") strip from 1 length. Sew strips to 1 side of full panel.

3. Layer backing, batting, and quilt top; baste. Quilt as desired. Quilt shown was outline-quilted with dark gold pearl cotton in large utility stitches.

4. Make 190" of French-fold binding. Add binding to quilt.

Quilt Top Assembly Diagram

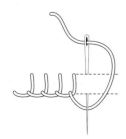

Blanket-Stitch Diagram

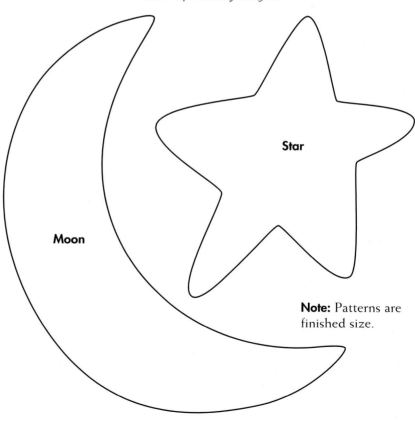

Moon

Star

Note: Patterns are finished size.

Mary's Graduation Quilt

As graduation day for her daughter approached, Marianne started planning how to commemorate the event in fabric. "At Mary's reception on graduation day, guests selected premade blocks from the design wall and wrote their well-wishes," says Marianne. "I finished the quilt in time for Mary to take it off to college to keep her warm. When I washed the quilt recently, I noticed she has added in one corner, 'One year later and I still sleep well.' "

Finished Size: 69¾" x 95¼"   Blocks: 59 (9") Puss in the Corner Blocks

materials

30 fat quarters* assorted batik prints
5½ yards off-white fabric
¾ yard blue print for binding
6 yards fabric for backing
Full-size batting
*Fat quarter = 18" x 22"

cutting

Measurements include ¼" seam allowance. Cut crosswise strips unless otherwise noted.

From assorted batik prints, cut:

- 59 sets (2 from each fabric) of:
  - 4 (3½") squares (A).
  - 4 (2") squares (D).
- From remainder, cut 22"-long strips, ranging from 1½" to 4½" wide for border.

From off-white, cut:

- 22 (6½"-wide) strips. Cut strips into 59 (6½") squares (B) and 236 (2" x 6½") rectangles (C).
- 2 (14"-wide) strips. Cut strips into 5 (14") squares. Cut squares in quarters diagonally to make 20 quarter-square side setting triangles.
- 1 (7¼"-wide) strip. Cut strip into 2 (7¼") squares. Cut squares in half diagonally to make 4 half-square corner setting triangles.

From blue print, cut:

- 9 (2¼"-wide) strips for binding.

block assembly

1. Using diagonal seams, join 1 A square to opposite corners of 1 B square (*Diagram 1*). Trim and open out (*Diagram 2*).

2. Join 1 A square to each remaining corner (*Diagram 3*). Trim and open out (*Diagram 4*).

3. Referring to *Block Assembly Diagram*, add 2 C strips to opposite sides of block. Add 1 D square to each end of 2 C strips. Add to top and bottom of block to complete block.

4. Make 59 Puss in the Corner Blocks (*Block Diagram*). →

Trim.   Stitch.

Diagram 1

Diagram 2

Diagram 3

Diagram 4

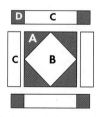

Block Assembly Diagram

Block Diagram

quilt assembly

1. Lay out blocks and setting triangles as shown in photo. Join into diagonal rows. Join rows to complete quilt.

2. Join random-width 22"-long batik strips into strip sets about 12" wide. Press seams to 1 side. From strip sets, cut 3½"-wide segments. Join segments to form 2 (3½" x 89¾") side borders, 2 (3½" x 64½") top and bottom borders, and 4 (3½") border corner squares.

3. Join 3½" x 89¾" borders to quilt sides. Sew border corners to ends of remaining borders, turning so that strips change direction at each corner. Sew borders to quilt top and bottom.

quilting and finishing

1. Divide backing fabric into 2 (3-yard) lengths. Cut 1 piece in half lengthwise. Sew 1 narrow panel to each side of wide panel. Press seam allowances toward narrow panels.

2. Layer backing, batting, and quilt top; baste. Quilt as desired. Quilt shown was meander-quilted in sashing and setting triangles only.

3. Join 2¼"-wide blue print strips into 1 continuous piece for straight-grain French-fold binding. Add binding to quilt.

tips for signature quilts

- Use light-value fabric for signature area so that writing will show.
- Press shiny side of freezer-paper pieces to signature areas on back of block. Paper stabilizes fabric for writing and peels off easily later.
- For signatures, buy pens that are permanent and specially designed for fabric use. Beware of Sharpie® pens; they write well, but oily outline develops around ink over time.
- Mail blocks (with pen and stamped return envelope) to friends and family who live too far away to attend graduation.
- Don't think of graduation quilts as heirloom quilts. If quilt is in shreds at end of four years, it's served its purpose well!

Quilt Top Assembly Diagram

Quilt designed and made by Marianne Fons, Liz Porter, and Marty Freed; quilted by Kathy Herzberg

USA Forever

One fall, Liz, Marianne, and friend Marty Freed took a seminar on Civil War quilt history from Barbara Brackman. Another participant, Terry Thompson, inspired them with a flag design she was working on. "We modified the flag, included a star border, and had fun with Terry's tube lettering technique," says Marianne.

Finished size: 42½" x 51"   Blocks: 18 (6") Sawtooth Stars plus Center Flag

materials

¼ yard tan print for star centers

¼ yard each 12 to 18 light prints for star backgrounds and stripes

⅛ yard each 18 dark prints: 7 blue, 7 red, and 4 gold for star blocks

⅛ yard each 7 assorted red prints for stripes

¾ yard red print for setting triangles

1 yard dark blue-and-gold star print for flag borders and binding

12½" square light blue print for star field

⅛ yard unbleached muslin for appliquéd stars

⅛ yard gold solid fabric or ½"-wide packaged bias for lettering

1¾ yards fabric for backing

cutting

Measurements include ¼" seam allowance. Cut crosswise strips unless otherwise noted:

From tan print, cut:

- 2 (3½"-wide) strips. Cut strips into 18 (3½") squares for Sawtooth Star centers (D).

From assorted light prints, cut:

- 2 (2" x 28½") strips from 2 different light prints for flag stripes.
- 4 (2" x 16½") strips from 4 different light prints for flag stripes.

- 18 sets of 4 (2") squares (C).
- 18 sets of 4 (2" x 3½") rectangles (A).

From assorted dark prints, cut:

- 18 sets of 8 (2") squares (B).

From assorted red prints, cut:

- 3 (2" x 28½") strips from 3 different prints for flag stripes.
- 4 (2" x 16½") strips from 4 different prints for flag stripes.

From red print, cut:

- 2 (9¾"-wide) strips. Cut strips into 8 (9¾") squares. Cut squares in quarters diagonally to make 32 quarter-square side setting triangles.
- 1 (5⅛"-wide) strip. Cut strip into 4 (5⅛") squares. Cut squares in half diagonally to make 8 half-square corner setting triangles.

From dark blue-and-gold star print, cut:

- 4 (3½"-wide) strips. Cut strips into 2 (3½" x 28½") strips and 2 (3½" x 26") strips for flag borders.
- 5 (2¼"-wide) strips for binding.

From muslin, cut:

- 1 large and 6 small stars, using patterns on page 54 and adding ³⁄₁₆" seam allowance.

sawtooth star block assembly

1. Referring to *Diagonal Seams Diagrams,* place a dark B on 1 end of a light A, with right sides facing. Stitch along the diagonal. Trim excess and press. Repeat on other end. Make 4 matching A/B units.

2. Referring to *Sawtooth Star Block Assembly Diagram,* lay our 4 A/B units, 4 Cs, and 1 D. Mix light background as desired. Join into rows; join rows to complete block.

3. Make 18 Sawtooth Star Blocks (*Sawtooth Star Block Diagram*). ———➤

Diagonal Seams Diagrams

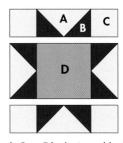

Sawtooth Star Block Assembly Diagram

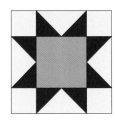

Sawtooth Star Block Diagram

Quilt designed and made by Liz Porter, Marianne Fons, and Marty Freed

flag assembly

1. Turn under and press or baste large and small star seam allowances. Referring to photo on page 53, machine-topstitch 1 large and 6 small white stars on light blue square.

2. Prepare and add gold lettering to light blue square (see "Letter Perfect" on opposite page).

3. Referring to *Flag Assembly Diagram,* join 4 red and 4 light 2" x 16½" strips, alternating colors. Add light blue square to left end.

4. Join 3 red print and 2 light print 2" x 28½" strips. Add to bottom of previous unit to complete flag.

5. Add 1 (3½" x 28½") dark blue border to quilt top and bottom. Add 1 (3½" x 26") border to each side.

border assembly

1. Arrange stars around flag as desired. For top and bottom borders, join 6 red side setting triangles and 2 corner setting triangles as shown in *Border Assembly Diagram.* Join into diagonal rows; join rows to complete border. Add to top and bottom of quilt.

2. Make side borders in similar manner, joining 6 red side setting triangles to 3 stars (no corner triangles), referring to *Quilt Top Assembly Diagram.* Join into diagonal rows; join rows to complete borders. Add to quilt sides.

3. Referring to *Corner Assembly Diagram,* add 2 red side setting triangles and 1 red corner triangle as shown to 1 star. Make 4 corner units and add to quilt, as shown in *Quilt Top Assembly Diagram.*

quilting and finishing

1. Layer backing, batting, and quilt top; baste. Quilt as desired. Quilt shown is machine-quilted. Flag has wave stitched through each stripe, and star field is outline-quilted to fill area. The words with stars between them appear in blue border: "America, Land of the free, Home of the brave. Give me liberty or give me death." The star border has a grid.

2. Join 2¼"-wide blue-and-gold star strips into 1 continuous piece to make approximately 5½ yards of French-fold straight-grain binding. Add binding to quilt.

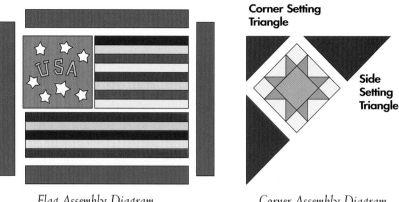

Flag Assembly Diagram

Corner Setting Triangle

Side Setting Triangle

Corner Assembly Diagram

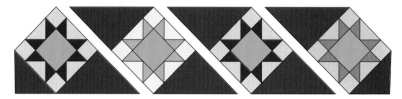

Border Assembly Diagram

Quilt Top Assembly Diagram

Large Star

Small Star

letter perfect

Save pieces of binding left over from a quilt to add words to your quilts. Either straight-grain strips or bias will work with this tube lettering technique.

This appliqué technique is easy since you use only straight machine stitching, not zigzag. And because you use binding to form your letters, there are no raw edges to turn under or to cover up.

A

Preparing the Strips

If you are making the lettering strips from scratch, simplify the technique by using a bias-strip maker that automatically folds over both raw edges ¼". Available in several sizes at fabric stores, it works the same for bias or straight-grain strips.

1. Rotary-cut 1½"-wide strips. Cut point at tip of each strip.

2. Set iron on cotton with no steam (to prevent burning your fingers). Pull pointed end of fabric strip through bias tool. Slowly and gently pull strip through tool, pressing folded edge as you pull *(Photo A)*. If fabric is resistant to creasing, spray it with mist of water or spray starch.

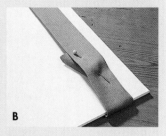

B

3. Wrap each pressed strip around piece of cardboard and pin to secure *(Photo B)*. This will keep folds in place until you are ready to use strip.

Laying out the Letters

Arrange the words on your quilt in an informal, freehand style.

1. Pin first letter in place.

C

2. Use continuous strip for each letter whenever possible. When you need to make turn, fold corners to create pleat *(Photo C)*. Some letters will require an extra strip here and there, such as middle bar in letter E.

3. Lay out all letters in all words before sewing to ensure they will fit.

Sewing the Letters

Use matching thread to machine-topstitch the letters close to the edge *(Photo D)*. The fewer times you stop and start, the cleaner your stitching will look. Try using quilter's pins to keep the edges turned under and to poke back any edges that pop out as you are sewing. Start sewing on the long side of the letter and experiment until the continuous line becomes easier. Your finished letter should have all the edges and the pleats stitched securely to the foundation fabric *(Photo E)*.

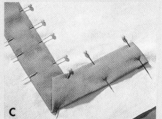

D

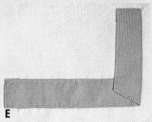

E

Suitable for Dad

Instead of giving Dad another tie this year, why not make use of his old ones?
Old-fashioned string piecing makes quick work of block assembly,
and you can accent the quilt with vintage buttons.

Finished Size: 22" x 22"   Blocks: 16 (5½") Blocks

Quilt designed and made by Liz Porter

materials

⅝ yard muslin for block
  foundations
14" square each of 2 wool tweed
  fabrics
4 or more neckties
9 buttons
26" square fabric for backing
26" square batting or flannel

cutting

Measurements include ¼" seam
allowance.

From muslin, cut:

- 3 (6"-wide) strips. Cut strips into
  16 (6") foundation squares.

From each wool fabric, cut:

- 4 (6⅜") squares. Cut squares in half
  diagonally to make 8 half-square
  triangles of each fabric.

For each necktie:

- Open back seam (*Photo A*). Remove
  interfacing and cut away lining at
  ends of tie. Open out tie and press
  flat. Cut into 1½" to 2½"-wide
  assorted strips.

block assembly

1. Fold 1 muslin square in half diagonally and crease.
2. Pin wool triangle right side up to
1 triangular half of muslin square, aligning corners. Place 1 tie strip along diagonal edge of wool triangle, with right
sides facing and raw edges aligned.
Stitch through all layers along diagonal
crease of muslin square (*Photo B*). Open
out tie strip and press seam (*Photo C*).
3. Place second tie strip atop first strip,
with right sides facing and raw edges
aligned; stitch (*Photo D*). Open out tie
strip (*Photo E*). Continue adding strips in
this manner until muslin square is

covered (*Photo F*). Trim outer edges
even with muslin square (*Photo G*).
4. Make 16 blocks (*Photo H*).

quilt assembly

1. Lay out blocks in 4 horizontal rows
of 4 blocks each.
2. Join blocks into rows. Join rows.
3. With right sides facing, position quilt
top on quilt back and pin around

perimeter. Stitch around quilt top, leaving 4" opening for turning. Trim corners
diagonally to reduce bulk.
4. Turn quilt right side out through
opening and press. Slipstitch opening
closed.
5. Stitch button at each intersection
where 4 blocks meet.
6. If desired, add hanging sleeve to quilt
back.

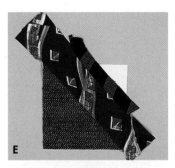

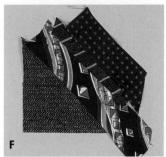

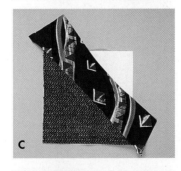

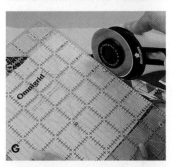

 Going back to **school** in the **fall** isn't just for kids. We can all **learn** some-thing and improve our **abilities!**

So now is a good time

for quilters to **think** about learning new **skills.**  The projects in this chapter alone will  teach you a wealth of quilting **techniques.**

String Spiderweb

Marion Roach Watchinski made "String Spiderweb" for her son to take to college. "I love plaids and scrap quilts," she says, "and I wanted something dark enough to hide spills. I rarely machine-quilt, but since I expect this quilt to be manhandled, it seemed the smart thing to do."

Finished Size: 70" x 84"

materials

26 (¼-yard) cuts assorted dark plaids and stripes

2½ yards dark red print for setting blocks and binding

5½ yards fabric for backing

Twin-size batting

cutting

Measurements include ¼" seam allowance. Cut crosswise strips unless otherwise noted.

From each ¼ yard of dark plaids and stripes, cut:

• 5 (1¾" x 42") strips, for a total of 130 strips.

From dark red print, cut:

• 9 (6¾"-wide) strips.

• 8 (2¼"-wide) strips for binding.

block assembly

1. Join 5 assorted dark plaid strips into a set *(Diagram 1)*. Make 26 strip sets.

2. To rotary-cut triangles, make initial cut, using 60° angle on your ruler *(Diagram 2)*. Discard end piece. Make subsequent cuts, using 60° angle on your ruler *(Diagram 3)*. Cut strip sets into 216 pieced equilateral triangles.

3. In same manner, cut 6¾"-wide dark red strips into 78 equilateral triangles.

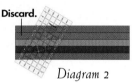

Diagram 1

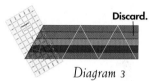

Discard.

Diagram 2

Discard.

Diagram 3

quilt assembly

1. Referring to *Quilt Top Assembly Diagram*, lay out triangles for Row 1. Join into row, matching seams. Make 4 of Row 1.

2. Repeat Step 1 to make 4 of Row 2, 3 of Row 3, and 3 of Row 4.

3. Lay out rows as shown in *Quilt Top Assembly Diagram*. Join rows, matching seams, to complete quilt.

4. Use 24"-long ruler to trim excess triangles along sides of quilt, leaving ¼" seam allowance.

⟶

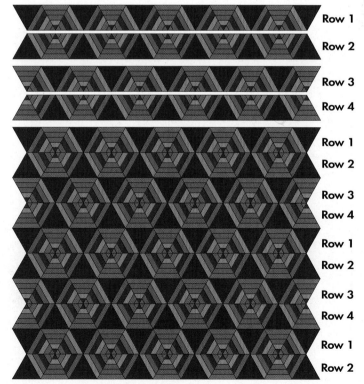

Row 1
Row 2
Row 3
Row 4
Row 1
Row 2
Row 3
Row 4
Row 1
Row 2
Row 3
Row 4
Row 1
Row 2

Quilt Top Assembly Diagram

quilting and finishing

1. Divide backing fabric into 2 (2¾-yard) lengths. Cut 1 piece in half lengthwise. Sew 1 narrow panel to each side of wide panel. Press seam allowance toward narrow panels.

2. Layer backing, batting, and quilt top; baste. Quilt as desired. Quilt shown was quilted in-the-ditch between triangles.

3. Join 2¼"-wide dark red strips into 1 continuous piece for straight-grain French-fold binding. Add binding to quilt.

Quilt made by Marion Roach Watchinski

Trace, scan, or photocopy this quilt label to finish your quilt.

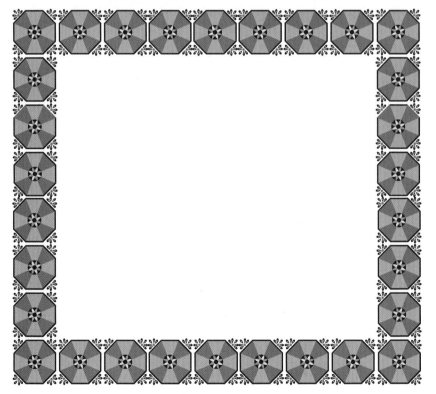

Quilt Label

Country Barns

Cozy plaids and red barns bring home a harvest-time theme.
Diagonal seams make quick work of the trees, and the Log Cabin
borders are a quick-pieced breeze.

Finished Size: 42½" x 52½" Blocks: 4 (14" x 10") Barns,   4 (3" x 6") Small Tree Blocks,
10 (6" x 7½") Large Tree Blocks,   32 (5¼") Log Cabin Blocks

materials

3½ yards total of assorted cream and
    light pastel plaid and print fabric
    scraps for sky areas of Barn Blocks
    and light side of Log Cabin Blocks
4 (4¼" x 5¾") pieces dark red
    fabric for barn sides
4 (4" x 15") pieces bright red fabric for
    barn fronts
1 (3" x 20") piece black plaid fabric for
    barn loft doors
⅛ yard navy stripe for silos
4 (5" x 11") pieces medium to dark
    plaids for barn roofs
1 (2" x 13") piece medium plaid for silo
    tops
½ yard total of 8 assorted green plaid
    and print fabric scraps for trees
⅛ yard or scraps brown print for tree
    trunks
2 (1¼" x 42") strips red fabric for Log
    Cabin centers
20 (1¼" x 42") strips assorted medium
    and dark plaids for dark sides of Log
    Cabin Blocks
1⅝ yards fabric for backing
¾ yard fabric for binding
45" x 60" crib-size batting
Rotary cutter, ruler, and cutting mat
Template material

general instructions

Measurements for cutting include ¼"
seam allowances. Cut all strips crosswise. Make templates for barn, using
patterns F, G, and I. Cutting and piecing instructions for Barn, Small Tree,
Large Tree, and Log Cabin Blocks are
given in separate sections. Extra pieces
for quilt assembly are given in each section. To achieve the scrappy look of the
quilt, include a variety of different fabrics in each block. For example, for a

Small Tree Block, cut each sky piece
from a different light fabric and each
tree piece from a different green fabric.

MAKING BARN BLOCKS
cutting

Note: Liz reversed Templates G and I
to cut pieces for 1 barn so that it would
face in opposite direction from other
3 barns.

From each dark red, cut:
- 1 (4¼" x 5¾") rectangle for barn
  side (A).

**From each bright red, cut matching
    pieces:**
- 2 (3" x 4¼") rectangles for barn
  fronts (B).
- 1 (1¾" x 3") rectangle for barn
  front (D).
- 1 (3⅜") square. Cut square in half
  diagonally to make 2 barn front
  triangles (E).

From black plaid, cut:
- 4 barn loft doors (F), using patterns
  on page 67.

From navy stripe, cut:
- 4 silo short sides (I), using template
  on page 67.
- 4 (1¾" x 8") rectangles for silo long
  side (J).

From each plaid for roofs, cut:
- 1 roof (G), using template on page 67.

**From medium plaid scrap for silo
    tops, cut:**
- 4 (1¾" x 3") rectangles (K).

**From assorted light pastel plaids and
    prints, cut:**
- 2 (3¾") squares from 2 different light
  fabrics that contrast with each other.
  Cut each square in quarters diagonally
  to make 4 triangles (C) of each fabric.
  You will only need 2 triangles of each
  type to make 1 Barn.

- 2 (3⅜") squares. Cut squares in half
  diagonally to make 4 sky (E) triangles.
  You will use 1 triangle per Barn.
- 2 (4⅝") squares. Cut squares in half
  diagonally to make 4 sky triangles
  (H). You will use 1 triangle per Barn.
- 4 (3" x 12") rectangles for sky (M).
- 4 (1¾" x 3") rectangles for sky (D).
- 8 (1¾") squares to make sky (L).

piecing

1. Referring to *Barn Block Diagram*, join
2 triangles (C) from 2 different fabrics
into a square with matching triangles
opposite each other to make door. Add
red barn front (D) rectangle to top of
door to complete barn front door unit.
2. Join barn side (A), barn front (B),
door unit, and barn front (B) into row.
3. Make barn top front unit by stitching
1 red triangle (E) to opposite sides of
barn loft door (F).
4. Stitch light triangle (E) to side of
short silo piece (I) to create triangle. Sew
triangle to side of barn top front unit.
5. Join roof (G) to other side of barn
front unit. Sew triangle (H) to other
slanted side of roof (G) to complete row.
6. Stitch barn roof row to top of barn
side/front row. Add long silo piece (J) to
side of joined rows.
7. Use diagonal-seams method to
create Goose Chase unit for silo top
from 1 plaid piece (K) and 2 light

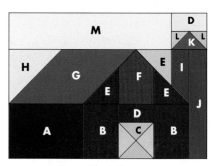

Barn Block Diagram

squares (L). Sew light rectangle (D) to pointed end of silo top unit. Add rectangle (M) to side of silo top unit to complete row. Join row to top edge of barn rows to complete block.
8. Make total of 4 Barn Blocks.

MAKING SMALL TREE BLOCKS
cutting
From 3 different green fabrics, cut:
- 4 (2" x 3½") rectangles from each fabric for a total of 12 rectangles.

From 8 different light fabrics, cut:
- 4 (2") squares from 6 fabrics for a total of 24 squares.
- 4 (1½" x 2") rectangles from 2 fabrics for a total of 8 rectangles.

From brown print, cut:
- 4 (1½" x 2") rectangles for tree trunks.

From remaining light fabrics, cut the following spacers to be used for all Small Tree Blocks:
- 4 (2½" x 3½") rectangles.
- 2 (3½" x 4½") rectangles.

piecing
1. Referring to *Diagonal Seams Diagrams*, make 1 Goose Chase unit by using diagonal-seams method to add light 2" square to each short side of green rectangle. Repeat to make a total of 12 Goose Chase units.
2. Sew 1½" x 2" light rectangle to opposite sides of brown tree trunk rectangle. Repeat to make 4 units.
3. Referring to *Small Tree Block Diagram*, join rows to complete block. Make 4 Small Tree Blocks.
4. Stitch 2½" x 3½" spacer rectangle to top and bottom edges of 2 Small Tree Blocks.
5. Stitch 3½" x 4½" spacer rectangle to top edge of 2 Small Tree Blocks.

Diagonal Seams Diagrams

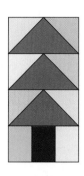

Small Tree Block Diagram

MAKING LARGE TREE BLOCKS
cutting
From each of 5 assorted green fabrics, cut the following pieces from different fabrics:
- 2 (2" x 3½") rectangles for top row of tree.
- 2 (2" x 4½") rectangles for second row of tree.
- 2 (2" x 5½") rectangles for third row of tree.
- 2 (2" x 6½") rectangles for fourth row of tree.

From each of 10 assorted light fabrics, cut the following pieces from different fabrics:
- 2 (2" x 3½") rectangles for first row of tree.
- 2 (2" x 3") rectangles for second row of tree.
- 2 (2" x 2½") rectangles for third row of tree.
- 2 (2") squares for fourth row of tree.
- 2 (2" x 3") rectangles for trunk row.

From brown fabric, cut:
- 10 (1½" x 2") rectangles for tree trunks.

From remaining light fabrics, cut the following spacers to be used for all Large Tree Blocks:
- 8 (1¾" x 6½") rectangles.
- 6 (3" x 6½") rectangles.

piecing
1. Referring to *Large Tree Block Diagram*, make tree top row, using diagonal-seams method to stitch 1 (2" x 3½") light rectangle to each short side of 2" x 3½" green rectangle. In a similar manner, make second, third, and fourth tree rows, using appropriate green and light pieces.
2. Make tree trunk row by joining 1 light trunk rectangle to opposite sides of brown trunk rectangle.
3. Join the 4 tree rows and trunk row. Make 10 Large Tree Blocks.
4. Stitch 1¾" x 6½" spacer rectangle to top and bottom edges of 4 Large Tree Blocks.
5. Stitch 3" x 6½" spacer rectangle to top edge of 3 Large Tree Blocks and to bottom edge of remaining 3 Large Tree Blocks.

Large Tree Block Diagram

MAKING LOG CABIN BLOCKS
cutting
Cutting instructions are for making 32 Log Cabin Blocks. To cut pieces for light logs, you will need ⟶

approximately 16 (1¼" x 42") strips of assorted light fabrics. To cut pieces for dark logs, you will need approximately 20 (1¼" x 42") strips of assorted medium and dark plaid fabrics. To piece 1 block, you will need 1 of each type piece. Log pieces are numbered in order that they are added to block center. Cut and assemble pieces so that there is variety in light and dark areas of blocks.

From 1¼"-wide red strips, cut:

• 32 (1¼") center squares #1.

From 1¼"-wide light strips, cut 32 each of the following pieces:

• 1¼" square for #2.

• 2"-long rectangle for #3.

• 2¾"-long rectangle for #6.

• 3½"-long rectangle for #7.

• 4¼"-long rectangle for #10.

• 5"-long rectangle for #11.

From 1¼"-wide medium and dark strips, cut 32 each of the following pieces:

• 2"-long rectangle for #4.

• 2¾"-long rectangle for #5.

• 3½"-long rectangle for #8.

• 4¼"-long rectangle for #9.

• 5"-long rectangle for #12.

• 5¾"-long rectangle for #13.

piecing

1. Referring to *Log Cabin Block Diagram*, add logs in numerical order (#2 to #13) around center red square (#1). After adding each piece, press seam allowances away from center square. Each block should measure 5¾" square, including seam allowances, and will finish 5¼" square.

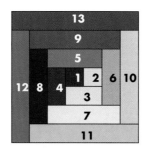

Log Cabin Block Diagram

2. Repeat to make total of 32 Log Cabin Blocks.

assembling quilt top

1. Referring to *Quilt Top Assembly Diagram*, lay out and join Barn, Small Tree, and Large Tree blocks in 4 horizontal rows. Join rows.

Quilt Top Assembly Diagram

2. From variety of light fabrics, cut assorted length 1½"-wide strips and join them into 2 rows, each 32½" long. Stitch 1 row to top and bottom of quilt top.
3. Join 8 Log Cabin Blocks for side border, turning blocks as shown in *Quilt Top Assembly Diagram.* Repeat for other side border. Stitch borders to sides of quilt. Join 8 Log Cabin blocks for top and for bottom borders; stitch borders to quilt.
Note: For the top and bottom Log Cabin rows, you will need to cut 2 (1" x 5¾") spacers. Add 1 spacer between 2 Log Cabin Blocks in the top row and 1 spacer between 2 Log Cabin Blocks in the bottom row as shown in *Quilt Top Assembly Diagram.*

quilting and finishing

1. Layer backing, batting, and quilt top; baste. Quilt as desired.
2. From binding fabric, make approximately 200" of French-fold binding and add to quilt. Add hanging sleeve if desired.

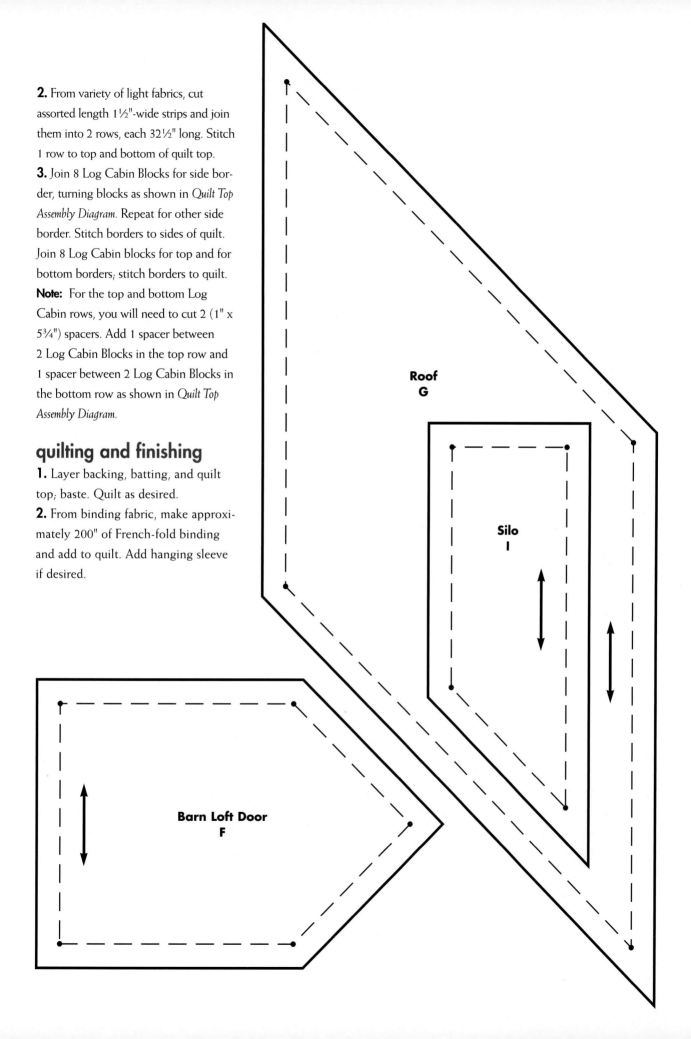

Roof
G

Silo
I

Barn Loft Door
F

Jack-o'-lanterns

Make a great lap quilt for fall or delight a child with a coverlet for his or her twin bed. Scary faces on pumpkins were originally meant to protect a house from evil spirits on Halloween, so you'll find some Bad Jacks among the Happy Jacks on this quilt.

Finished Size: 70½" x 88½"   Blocks: 12 (13½") Pumpkin Blocks

materials

12 assorted fat quarters* orange prints for pumpkins

12 assorted fat quarters* dark prints for pumpkin backgrounds

¼ yard dark print for sashing squares

¼ yard yellow solid for lit faces

⅛ yard green solid for stems

1 yard yellow-and-purple mottled print for sashing

1 yard black-and-jewel-tone checked fabric for pieced inner border (2¼ yards for unpieced borders), or see page 72 for instructions for making your own checked border

1½ yards black print #1 for pieced outer border (2¼ yards for unpieced borders)

¾ yard black print #2 for binding

5½ yards fabric for backing

Twin-size batting

*Fat quarter = 18" x 22"

cutting

Measurements include ¼" seam allowance. Unless noted, cut crosswise strips.

From each of 10 orange fat quarters, cut for Happy Jacks:

- 3 (2") squares (A).
- 4 (3½" x 5") rectangles (B).
- 2 (3⅞") squares. Cut squares in half diagonally to make 4 half-square triangles (C).
- 5 (2" x 3½") rectangles (D).
- 2 (3½") squares (G).
- 1 (1¼" x 2") rectangle (H).

From each of remaining 2 orange fat quarters, cut for Bad Jacks:

- 6 (2") squares (A).
- 2 (3⅞") squares. Cut squares in half diagonally to make 4 half-square triangles (C).
- 1 (1¼" x 2") rectangle (H).
- 1 (2" x 8") rectangle (I).
- 2 (5" x 6½") rectangles (J).
- 1 (3½" x 8") rectangle (K).

From dark fat quarters, cut:

- 12 sets for pumpkin background of:
  - 1 (2") square (A).
  - 1 (3½" x 5") rectangle (B).
  - 3 (3⅞") squares. Cut squares in half diagonally to make 6 half-square triangles (C). You will have 1 extra in each set.
  - 1 (3½" x 6½") rectangle (E).
- For unlit Happy Jack faces:
  - 5 sets (to match 5 backgrounds above) of 9 (2") A squares and 1 (1¼" x 2") H rectangle.
- For unlit Bad Jack faces:
  - 1 set (to match 1 background above) of 5 (2") A squares, 2 (2" x 3½") D rectangles, and 1 (1¼" x 2") H rectangle.

From dark print for sashing squares, cut:

- 1 (5"-wide) strip. Cut strip into 6 (5") sashing squares.

From yellow solid, cut:

- For lit Happy Jack face:
  - 5 sets of 9 (2") A squares and 1 (1¼" x 2") H rectangle.
- For lit Bad Jack faces:
  - 1 set of 5 (2") A squares, 2 (2" x 3½") D rectangles, and 1 (1¼" x 2") H rectangle.

From green solid, cut:

- 1 (3⅞"-wide) strip. Cut strip into 6 (3⅞") squares. Cut squares in half diagonally to make 12 F triangles.

From yellow-and-purple mottled print, cut:

- 6 (5"-wide) strips. Cut strips into 17 (5" x 14") sashing strips.

From black-and-jewel-tone checked fabric, cut:

- 7 (5"-wide) strips. Piece to make 2 (5" x 68") side border strips and 2 (5" x 59") top and bottom border strips, matching patterns. If you prefer unpieced borders, use alternate yardage and cut 4 (5"-wide) lengthwise strips. Trim to above lengths. If you cannot find checked fabric, see page 72 to make your own. $\longrightarrow$

From black print #1, cut:

- 8 (6½"-wide) strips. Piece to make 2 (6½" x 77") side outer border strips and 2 (6½" x 71") top and bottom outer border strips. If you prefer unpieced borders, use alternate yardage to cut 4 (6½"-wide) lengthwise strips.

From black print #2, cut:

- 9 (2¼"-wide) strips for binding.

Happy Jack block assembly

1. Choose 1 matching set each of pumpkin pieces, background pieces, and face pieces.

2. Referring to *Diagram 1*, join 1 background C triangle and 1 green F triangle to make a half-square triangle unit. Using diagonal seams, lay 1 background A square atop 1 F corner. Stitch diagonally as shown and trim excess. Press open to make stem unit. Add 1 B and 1 E as shown in *Happy Jack Block Assembly Diagram* to complete Row #1.

3. Using diagonal seams, join 1 face A square to 1 pumpkin D rectangle (*Diagram 2*). Make 2 units and 2 reversed units as shown. Join with 1 pumpkin D rectangle as shown in *Happy Jack Block Assembly Diagram* to make D strip. Join 1 background C triangle and 1 pumpkin C triangle to make half-square triangle unit. Make 4 units. Join 1 C unit to each end of D strip to make Row #2. Reserve remaining 2 C units for Row #4.

4. Join 1 pumpkin A to each side of 1 face A to make nose strip. Using diagonal seams, join 1 face A square to 1 side of 1 pumpkin B rectangle. Repeat as shown to make 1 reversed unit. Join 2 A/B units, nose strip, and 2 pumpkin Bs into Row #3.

5. Join 1 pumpkin H, 1 face H, and 1 pumpkin A square as shown to make mouth unit. Using diagonal seams, join 1 face A to 1 pumpkin G square (*Diagram 3*). Make 2 units as shown. Join with mouth unit and remaining C units to complete Row #4.

6. Join rows to complete block (*Happy Jack Block Diagram*).

7. Make 10 Happy Jack Blocks, 5 with unlit faces and 5 with lit faces.

Bad Jack block assembly

1. Make Row #1 as above.

2. Using diagonal seams, join 1

Diagram 1

Diagram 2

Diagram 3

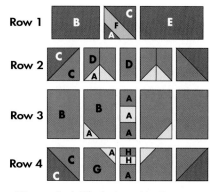

Happy Jack Block Assembly Diagram

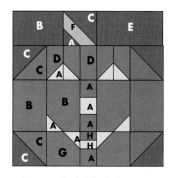

Happy Jack Block Diagram

pumpkin A square to each end of 1 face D rectangle (*Diagram 4*). Make 2 eye units. Join eye units to each side of 1 pumpkin A square, as shown in *Bad Jack Block Assembly Diagram*. Join 1 pumpkin I to top of strip. Join 1 background C and 1 pumpkin C to make a half-square triangle unit. Make 4 units. Add 1 C unit to each end of eye strip to complete Row #2. Reserve remaining C units for Row #4.

3. Using diagonal-seams method and referring to *Bad Jack Block Assembly Diagram*, Row #3, join 1 face A square to 1 pumpkin J. Repeat as shown. Join 1 face A, 1 pumpkin A, 1 face H, and 1 pump-kin H into a strip as shown to make 1 reversed unit. Join J units to each side to complete Row #3.

4. Using diagonal-seams method and referring to *Bad Jack Block Assembly*

Diagram, Row #4, join 1 face A square to each end of 1 pumpkin K. Join remaining C units to each end to complete Row #4.

5. Join rows to complete block.

6. Make 1 Bad Jack with unlit face and 1 with lit face.

quilt assembly

1. Using photo on page 73 as guide, arrange blocks in 4 rows of 3 blocks each. Alternate blocks in each row with sashing strips and join. Alternate 3 sashing strips and 2 sashing squares and join. Make 3 sashing strip rows.

2. Alternate block rows with sashing strip rows and join.

3. Add 68"-long checked borders to opposite sides of quilt top. Join remaining 59"-long checked borders to quilt top and bottom. Or see page 72 to make pieced checked borders.

4. In a similar manner, add black borders to quilt.

quilting and finishing

1. Divide backing fabric into 2 (2¾-yard) lengths. Cut 1 piece in half lengthwise. Sew 1 narrow panel to each side of wide panel. Press seam allowance toward narrow panels.

2. Layer backing, batting, and quilt top; baste. Quilt as desired. Quilt shown was machine-quilted around each face and in curved lines to suggest pumpkin ridges. Background area is filled with pumpkin leaf and vine motifs. Checked border is quilted in-the-ditch of pattern.

3. Join 2¼"-wide black print #2 strips into 1 continuous piece for straight-grain French-fold binding. Add binding to quilt. ⟶

Diagram 4

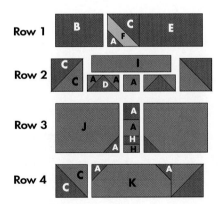

Bad Jack Block Assembly Diagram

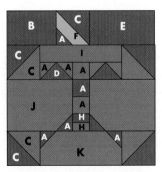

Bad Jack Block Diagram

making inner checked border

If you can't find a checked fabric that is the right size
for this quilt, make your own!

¾ yard black solid
¼ yard each of 4 jewel-tone prints

1. Cut 12 (2"-wide) strips from black solid. Cut
3 (2"-wide) strips from each jewel-tone print.
2. Referring to *Strip Set A Diagram,* join 2 black
strips and 1 jewel-tone strip to make 1 Strip Set
A. Make 4 strip sets, 1 from each jewel-tone
print.
3. Referring to *Strip Set B Diagram,* join 2 jewel-
tone strips and 1 black strip to make 1 Strip Set
B. Make 4 strip sets, 1 from each jewel-tone
print.
4. Cut 84 (2"-wide) segments from Strip Set A
and 84 (2"-wide) segments from Strip Set B.
5. Referring to *Checkerboard Assembly Diagrams,*
alternate segments and join to make 2 (45-unit)
side border strips, beginning and ending with
B segment. Join strips to make 2 (39-unit) top
and bottom borders, beginning and ending with
an A segment.

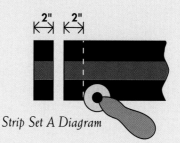

Strip Set A Diagram

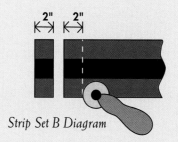

Strip Set B Diagram

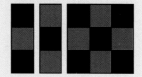
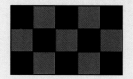

Checkerboard Assembly Diagrams

Fall **73**

Impressions of Fall

Peggy Mathews made this quilt with Benartex's 1997 challenge fabrics, Impressions. Her quilt, along with several others, toured selected quilt shops around the country. "Leaves are a recurrent theme in my quilts," says Peggy, "perhaps because of my New England background."

Finished Size: 39" x 39"

materials

24 assorted fall prints—½ yard yellow, ½ yard orange, ¼ yard each of 2 golds, ¼ yard each of 3 pinks, ¼ yard each of 2 reds, ¼ yard each of 4 purples, 1 (5" x 8") square each of 6 browns, and ¼ yard each of 5 greens

1¾ yards gray print for background and border

1¼ yards fabric for backing

Crib-size batting

cutting

Measurements include ¼" seam allowances. Pieces cut for large leaves have capital letters (A–H), and pieces for small leaves have lowercase letters (a–z, yy, zz). As you cut, label and store pieces in zip-top bags. Follow *Quilt Diagram* on page 76 and *Cutting Chart* at right to arrange pieces as shown.

From yellow, cut:
• 4 (1"-wide) strips for inner border.

From orange, cut:
• 4 (2¼"-wide) strips for binding.

From gold #1, cut:
• 2 (1⅞") squares for stem C sides.

From gray print, cut:
• 4 (3"-wide) strips for outer border.

Cutting Chart

Color	Leaf	2" squares	2⅜" squares cut into half-square triangles
yellow	A, j, q	19 (12A, 3j, 4q)	8 squares = 15 triangles (6A, 5j, 4q)
orange	H, l, s	19 (12H, 3l, 4s)	8 squares = 15 triangles (6H, 5l, 4s)
gold 1	f, o, w	10 (2f, 4o, 4w)	6 squares = 12 triangles (4f, 4o, 4w)
gold 2	E	11	3 squares = 6 triangles
pink 1	G, n	16 (12G, 4n)	5 squares = 9 triangles (6G, 3n)
pink 2	t	4	2 squares = 4 triangles
pink 3	C	12	3 squares = 5 triangles
red 1	B	12	3 squares = 6 triangles
red 2	p	4	2 squares = 4 triangles
purple 1	k, yy	7 (4k, 3yy)	5 squares = 9 triangles (4k, 5yy)
purple 2	i, v	8 (4i, 4v)	4 squares = 8 triangles (4i, 4v)
purple 3	c	4	2 squares = 4 triangles
purple 4	z	4	2 squares = 4 triangles
brown 1	a	4	2 squares = 4 triangles
brown 2	e	4	2 squares = 4 triangles
brown 3	u	4	2 squares = 4 triangles
brown 4	zz	4	2 squares = 4 triangles
brown 5	m	4	2 squares = 4 triangles
brown 6	d	4	2 squares = 4 triangles
green 1	D, h, y	19 (12D, 4h, 3y)	7 squares = 13 triangles (6D, 4h, 3y)
green 2	g, x	8 (4g, 4x)	4 squares = 8 triangles (4g, 4x)
green 3	F	12	3 squares = 6 triangles
green 4	r	4	2 squares = 3 triangles
green 5	b	4	2 squares = 4 triangles
gray		177 (9 strips)	4 strips = 64 squares = 127 triangles

- 4 (1⅞"-wide) strips. Cut strips into 68 (1⅞") squares for stem sides. Refer to *Cutting Chart* on page 74 for remainder of cutting.

block assembly

Closely follow *Quilt Diagram* throughout. There are 8 large leaves (A–H) and 28 small leaves (a–z, yy, zz).

1. Lay out all 2" squares (gray and colors) in position as shown in *Quilt Diagram.*

2. Join gray half-square triangles to colored half-square triangles to make triangle-squares. Place in position. Join colored half-square triangles as shown to make triangle-squares. Place in position.

3. Use *Paper Piecing Patterns* to paper-piece squares for Large Leaf Points. Photocopy or trace 8 of each pattern. For 2 side units, place gray square on back of pattern, right side up. Place colored square atop gray square, right sides facing, aligning ¼" from seam line. Stitch, open out, and trim to size.

For Large Leaf Point B square, place colored square on back of pattern, right side up. Place gray square atop colored square, right sides facing, aligning ¼" from seam line. Stitch, open out, and repeat on opposite side. Trim to size. Paper-piece 3 squares to form point for each large leaf. Place in position.

4. To piece ¾ blocks, join 2 half-square triangles to make a square (*¾-Block Diagram 1*). Place specified square atop unit, aligning outer edges (*¾-Block Diagram 2*). Stitch, trim, and open out (*¾-Block Diagram 3*). Piece all ¾ blocks and place in position.

5. Using diagonal-seams method and referring to *Stem Assembly Diagrams*, place 1 (1⅞") gray square atop 1 colored stem square, right sides facing. Stitch diago-

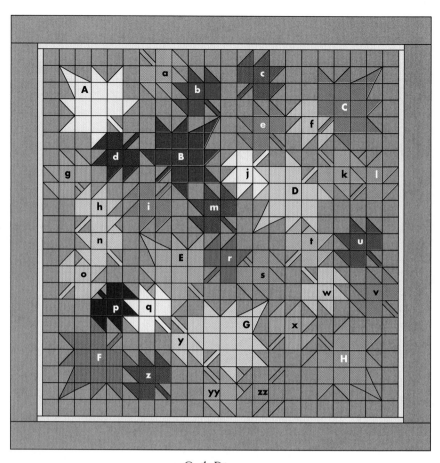

Quilt Diagram

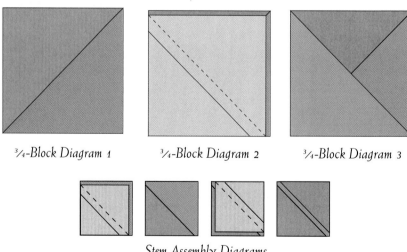

¾-Block Diagram 1 *¾-Block Diagram 2* *¾-Block Diagram 3*

Stem Assembly Diagrams

nally, trim, and open out. Repeat on opposite corner. There will be 1 (⅛"-wide) diagonal strip through the center forming stem. Piece all stem squares and place in position.

6. For half stems (leaves g, p, s) piece 1 stem block as in Step 5. Place colored square atop unit. Using diagonal-seams method, stitch, trim, and open out. Piece all half stems and place in position.

quilt assembly

1. When you are satisfied with placement of leaf components, join squares into rows. Join rows to complete quilt top.

2. Measure length of quilt. Trim yellow side borders to size and add to opposite sides of quilt top. Press seam allowance toward borders. Measure width of quilt, including borders. Trim remaining 2 yellow borders to size. Join to top and bottom of quilt.

3. Measure, trim, and add gray border to quilt as above.

quilting and finishing

1. Layer backing, batting, and quilt top; baste. Quilt as desired. Quilt shown was quilted in allover circles.

2. Join 2¼"-wide orange strips into 1 continuous piece for straight-grain French-fold binding. Add binding.

Quilt made by Peggy Mathews

Paper Piecing Patterns

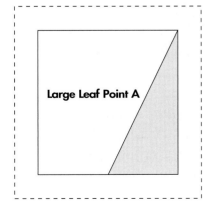

Large Leaf Point A

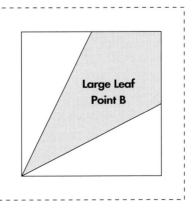

Large Leaf Point B

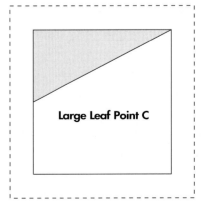

Large Leaf Point C

Abundant Blessings Wall Hanging

Jackie Leckband based her design for this wool quilt on an 1880s quilt handed down to her from her grandparents, Lucretia Comstock Wedge and Hugh Wedge. Both loved gardens and nature, so Jackie added the flower baskets and cherry branches. "To me," says Jackie, "this quilt represents love, work, abundance, and blessings."

Finished Size: 27" x 27"

materials

½ yard slate blue wool or felt for A and C

¾ yard black wool or felt for B and D

12" x 16" piece brown felt for hands, baskets, and circles

10" x 12" piece red felt for hearts, circles, pie shapes, flowers, and cherries

12" x 16" piece green felt for stems, leaves, tulip bases, and branches

8" x 10" piece maroon felt for pie shapes and roses

3" x 4" piece blue felt for center circle and tulip and rose flower centers

2" x 3" piece pink felt for flower centers

2" x 4" piece gold felt for flower centers

Paper or freezer paper for appliqué patterns

#8 gold pearl cotton

⅞ yard red-and-black check woven plaid for backing

Note: All seams and appliqué on quilt top are blanket-stitched with pearl cotton. Backing is folded to front to finish edges and stitched down with sewing thread. Quilt may be turned in any direction to hang. There will be enough backing left over to make a hanging sleeve.

cutting

From slate blue wool or felt, cut:

• 4 (6") squares (A).

• 1 (15") square (C).

From black wool or felt, cut:

• 4 (6" x 15") rectangles (B).

• 1 (10½") square (D).

Trace appliqué patterns from pages 80 and 81 onto freezer paper. Press paper patterns onto wool or felt and cut out the following appliqué shapes. Do not add seam allowances.

• Hearts and Hands center: 4 red hearts, 4 brown hands, 4 green leaves, 1 red small penny circle, 1 blue tiny penny circle, 4 maroon large pie shapes, and 4 red small pie shapes.

• Tulip Basket: 1 (⅜" x 1¼") green tulip stem, 2 (⅜" x 5") green stems, 3 red tulip flowers, 3 blue tulip centers, 3 green tulip bases, 4 green tulip leaves, and 1 brown tulip basket.

• Rose Basket: 1 (⅜" x 1½") green rose stem, 2 (⅜" x 5") green stems, 3 maroon outer roses, 3 (1") gold circles, 3 (⅝") pink circles, 3 (⅜") blue circles, 6 green leaves, and 1 brown rose basket.

• Cherry Branches: 2 green cherry stems, 2 each right and left green cherry branches (total of 4), 6 red cherries, and 12 green cherry leaves.

• Corner Blocks: 4 brown large circles and 4 red medium circles.

assembly

Note: Refer to photo at right and diagrams on page 80 throughout.

Center

1. Referring to *Blanket-Stitch Diagram* below, use gold pearl cotton to appliqué 1 red heart to center of each brown hand. Position hands on 10½" black square (D) and appliqué in place. ⟶

Blanket-Stitch Diagram

2. Add 4 leaves as shown. Backstitch leaf detail (*Backstitch Diagram*). Embroider cross detail at center of blue circle. Center and stitch blue circle on red circle. Stitch to center of square.

Flower Baskets

1. On 1 B rectangle, position tulips, stems, leaves, and basket as shown. Appliqué in place in following order: red tulip flowers, tulip bases, blue tulip center, green tulip stems, and leaves. Position basket over stem ends and stitch.

2. On 1 B rectangle, position roses, stems, leaves, and basket as shown in photo. Position and appliqué in following order: rose stems, maroon flowers, gold circles, pink circles, blue circles, leaves, and basket.

Cherry Branches

1. Place 3-stemmed piece in center of 1 B rectangle. Appliqué in place in following order: cherry stem, cherry branches, cherries, and leaves. Vary placement as desired.

2. Repeat for second cherry branch block.

Corners

1. Center 1 red circle on 1 brown circle and appliqué. Repeat to make 4 units.

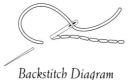

Backstitch Diagram

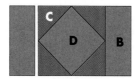

Diagram 1

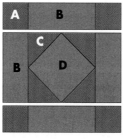

Block Assembly Diagram

2. Center each circle unit on each blue 6" square (A). Appliqué in place.

quilt top assembly

1. Center Hearts and Hands Block (D) diagonally on 15" slate blue square (C). Appliqué in place.

2. Position 1 red pie shape on top of

1 maroon pie shape and appliqué to 1 corner of C. Repeat for 4 corners.

3. Referring to *Diagram 1*, position rose basket block (B) on 1 side of C so that it overlaps on top by ¼". Blanket-stitch along overlap, securing both layers. Repeat on opposite side with tulip basket block (B).

4. Referring to *Block Assembly Diagram*, position 1 corner block (A) at 1 end of a cherry branch block (B). Overlap ¼", pin, and check that it aligns with center section seams. Blanket-stitch to secure. Repeat with opposite end. Repeat with remaining cherry branch block and corner blocks.

5. Overlap these border strips ¼" on top of center section and blanket-stitch.

quilting and finishing

1. Layer quilt top and backing. Quilt as desired. Quilt shown uses utility stitch, with outline-quilting around circles and inside triangle blocks.

2. Fold backing to front. Trim as necessary to form binding, fold over, and slipstitch in place, using regular sewing thread.

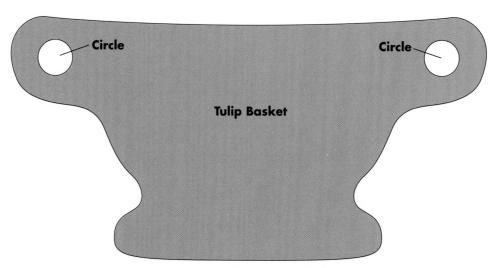

Circle

Circle

Tulip Basket

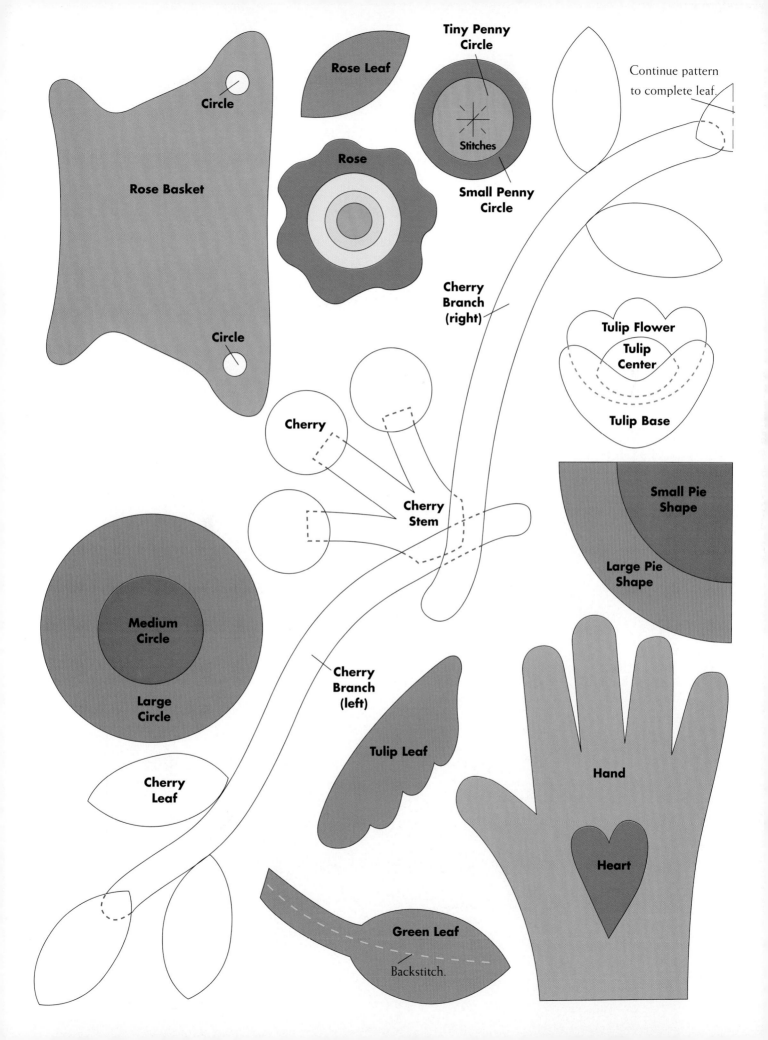

Rose Leaf

Tiny Penny Circle

Rose Basket

Circle

Rose

Stitches

Small Penny Circle

Continue pattern to complete leaf.

Cherry Branch (right)

Tulip Flower

Tulip Center

Circle

Cherry

Cherry Stem

Tulip Base

Small Pie Shape

Large Pie Shape

Medium Circle

Large Circle

Cherry Branch (left)

Cherry Leaf

Tulip Leaf

Hand

Heart

Green Leaf

Backstitch.

Bold and Batty

This stunning, whimsical quilt is the result of a round-robin border exchange. In round-robins, one person designs the center of a quilt, and friends add consecutive borders. "The center pumpkin block is my own design," says Mary Beth Bellah, of Charlottesville, Virginia. After Mary Beth made the center block, each member of the group supplied a border.

Finished Size: 44" x 44" (excluding rickrack trim)

materials

¾ yard candy corn novelty print for center background and candy corn border

6" x 10" pieces 4 different orange prints for pumpkin

3" x 5" piece green print for stem

1½ yards solid black for pumpkin face, bat border, candy corn border, and solid black border

1" x 2" piece gray print for eye accents

6" x 9" piece black plaid for cat

¼ yard yellow print for stairstep border

¼ yard black-and-purple print for stairstep border

1¼ yards light orange print for stairstep border and bat border

½ yard light yellow print for candy corn border

½ yard orange print for prairie point border

⅛ yard each of 10 assorted coordinating prints for prairie point border

3 yards Halloween novelty print for backing

Freezer paper for appliqué templates

Black bat plastic confetti (approximately 225 pieces)

Small black beads (approximately 225)

Metallic thread: orange, black, purple, yellow

5½ yards 1½"-wide black rickrack

Note: Measurements include ¼" seam allowances. Cut crosswise strips unless otherwise noted.

center pumpkin cutting and assembly

1. Cut 1 (15½") square from candy corn novelty print.

2. Make freezer-paper templates, using patterns A–M on pages 86 and 87. Adding ³⁄₁₆" for seam allowance, cut:
- 1 each A, B, D, E from 4 different orange prints.
- 1 C from green print.
- 2 F, 1 H, and 1 I from solid black.
- 2 G from gray.
- 1 each of J, K, L, and M from black plaid.

3. Referring to *Appliqué Diagram*, appliqué in alphabetical order.

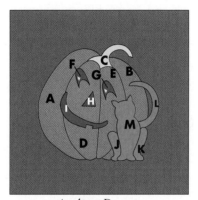

Appliqué Diagram

stairstep border cutting and assembly

From yellow print, cut:
- 2 (1½"-wide) strips.
- 1 (2½"-wide) strip.

From black-and-purple print, cut:
- 4 (1½"-wide) strips.

From light orange print, cut:
- 1 (4½"-wide) strip.
- 2 (3½"-wide) strips.
- 1 (2½"-wide) strip.
- 3 (1½"-wide) strips. Cut strips into 8 (1½") squares, 8 (1½" x 2½") rectangles, 8 (1½" x 3½") rectangles, and 8 (1½" x 4½") rectangles for corner blocks.

1. Join 1 (1½"-wide) black-and-purple strip to bottom of 4½"-wide orange strip. Press seam allowance

toward purple. Cut 16 (1½"-wide) segments (*Unit A Diagram*).

2. Join 1 (1½"-wide) black-and-purple strip to bottom of 1 (3½"-wide) orange strip. Join 1 (1½"-wide) yellow strip to black-and-purple strip. Repeat for second strip set. Cut 32 (1½"-wide) segments (*Unit B Diagram*).

3. Join 1 (1½"-wide) black-and-purple strip to bottom of 2½"-wide orange strip. Join 2½"-wide yellow strip to black-and-purple strip. Press seam allowances toward purple. Cut 16 (1½"-wide) segments (*Unit C Diagram*).

4. Join 2 B segments and 1 C segment as shown in *B/C/B Unit Diagram*. Make 16 B/C/B units. →

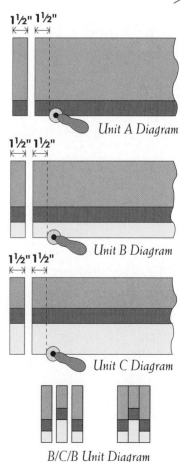

Unit A Diagram

Unit B Diagram

Unit C Diagram

B/C/B Unit Diagram

5. Referring to *Stairstep Border Assembly Diagram*, join 4 B/C/B units and 3 A segments to make border strip. Make 4 border strips.

6. To make corner blocks, join 2 (1½") orange squares as shown in *Corner Block Diagram*. Assembling pieces half-log cabin style, add 1 (1½" x 2½") orange rectangle to bottom and another to right side. Add 1 (1½" x 3½") orange rectangle to bottom and another to right side. Add 1 (1½" x 4½") orange rectangle to bottom and another to right side. Add 1 A unit to bottom, placing black square in lower right corner. Make 4 corner blocks.

7. Referring to *Quilt Top Assembly Diagram*, join 1 corner block to each end of 1 border strip. Repeat.

8. Join 2 shorter side border strips to center appliqué block. Add top and bottom borders.

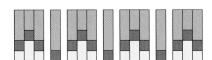

Stairstep Border Assembly Diagram

Corner Block Diagram

bat border cutting and assembly

1. Cut 4 (4"-wide) strips from light orange print. Center 1 border strip on each side of quilt and stitch. Miter corners.

2. Make freezer-paper templates, using bat patterns on page 86. Adding ³⁄₁₆" seam allowance, cut 8 full bats and 4 corner bats from solid black. Appliqué in place as shown in photo.

candy corn pieced border cutting and assembly

From solid black, cut:
- 2 (4¼"-wide) strips. Cut strips into 10 (4¼") squares. Cut squares in quarters diagonally to make 40 quarter-square triangles.

From candy corn print, cut:
- 2 (3⅞"-wide) strips. Cut strips into 20 (3⅞") squares. Cut squares in half diagonally to make 40 half-square triangles.

From light yellow prints, cut:
- 2 (4¼"-wide) strips. Cut strips into 10 (4¼") squares. Cut squares in quarters diagonally to make 40 quarter-square triangles.
- 1 (3½"-wide) strip. Cut strip into 8 (3½" x 7") rectangles for corners.

1. Join 1 black quarter-square triangle and 1 yellow quarter-square as shown in *Candy Corn Border Diagrams A and B*. Make 20 with black on left and 20 with black on right.

2. Join each black-and-yellow triangle to 1 candy corn half-square triangle. Make 40 units as shown.

3. Join 5 matching units as shown in *Candy Corn Border Diagram C*. Repeat to make 4 strips with candy corn print on right and 4 strips with print on left.

4. Join 1 right and 1 left strip as shown in *Candy Corn Border Diagram*

D. Add 1 yellow rectangle to each end to make 1 border strip. Make 4 border strips.

5. Cut 4 (1½"-wide) strips from solid black.

6. Referring to *Quilt Top Assembly Diagram*, center 1 black strip on each candy corn border and stitch.

7. Center 1 border strip on each side of quilt and stitch. Miter corners and trim excess.

prairie point border assembly

1. Cut 5 (2½"-wide) orange print strips. Join to make 4 (50"-long) borders.

2. Cut 60 (3½") squares from assorted prairie point fabrics. Referring to *Prairie Point Diagrams*, fold each square in quarters diagonally. With raw edges aligned, position prairie points along 1 edge of 1 orange border strip, overlapping ends ¼" to ⅜" to fit 40" of border length. Pin or baste in place. Make 3 more borders.

3. Pin orange borders in place and stitch. Miter corners and trim excess.

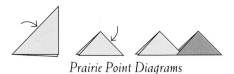

Prairie Point Diagrams

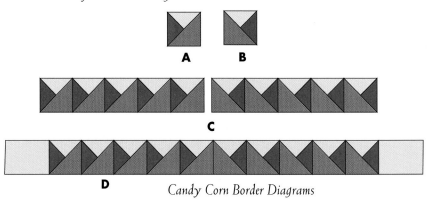

Candy Corn Border Diagrams

quilting and finishing

1. Divide backing fabric into 2 (1½-yard) lengths. Cut 1 piece in half lengthwise. Join 1 narrow panel to 1 side of wide panel. Press seam allowances toward narrow panel.

2. Layer backing, batting and quilt top; baste. Quilt as desired. Center of quilt shown was machine-outline-quilted around appliqué pieces with orange metallic thread. From appliqué center to first orange border is orange peel design worked in purple thread. Bats are outline-quilted, and orange area around bats is filled with echo quilting in black metallic thread. Candy corn border is outline quilted ¼" away from seams with yellow metallic thread in yellow areas and purple thread in dark areas. Black border has double row of quilting through center in black metallic thread. Prairie point border is unquilted.

3. For binding, cut 5 (2¼"-wide) strips from black fabric. Join to make approximately 5½ yards of French-fold straight-grain binding. Add binding to quilt.

4. Stitch down each prairie point with 1 bat confetti piece and 1 black bead (bead holds confetti piece in place). Stitch remaining confetti and beads as desired in outer border.

5. Tack rickrack to back of quilt as shown in photo at right so that half shows beyond edge. Fold cut ends under and tack to prevent fraying. →

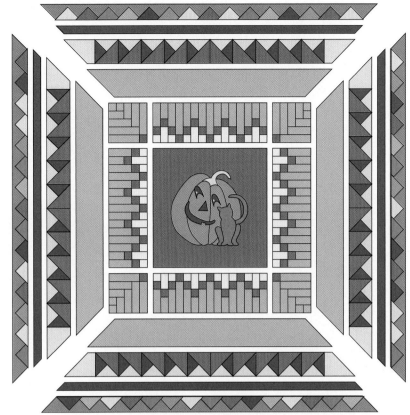

Quilt Top Assembly Diagram

Quilt made by Mary Beth Bellah; round-robin members include Linda Harker and Michele Johnson of Leavenworth, Kansas; Jolene Troupe of Fairbanks, Alaska; and Marilyn Tabachnick of Charlottesville, Virginia

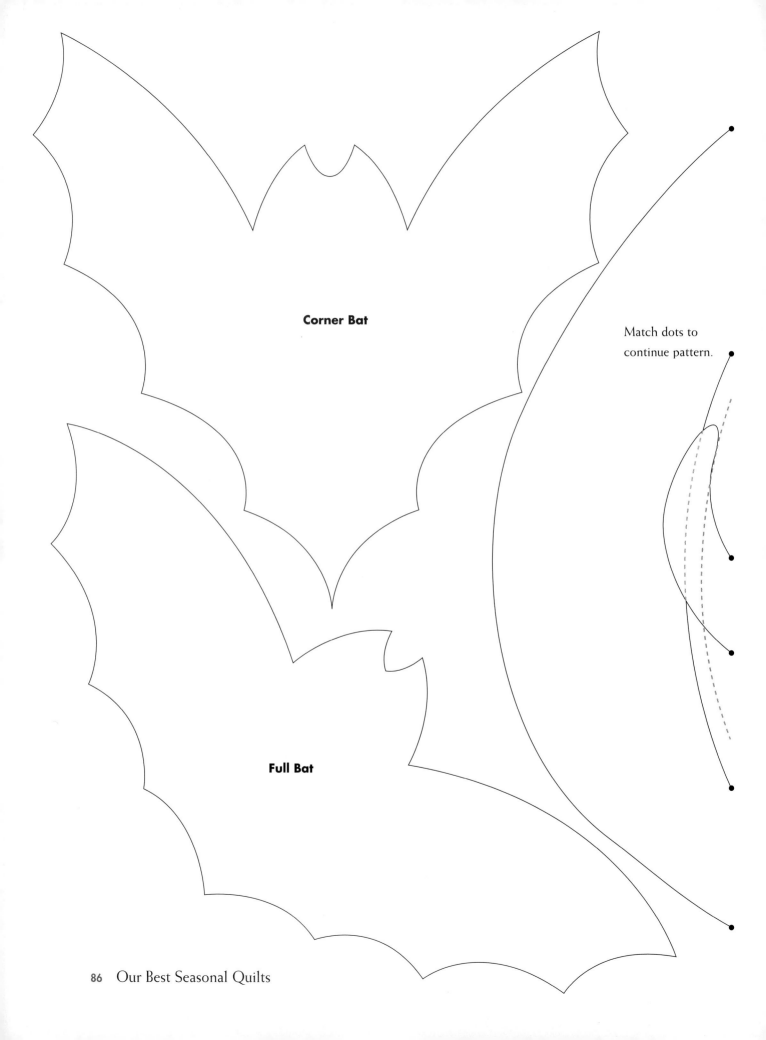

Corner Bat

Full Bat

Match dots to
continue pattern.

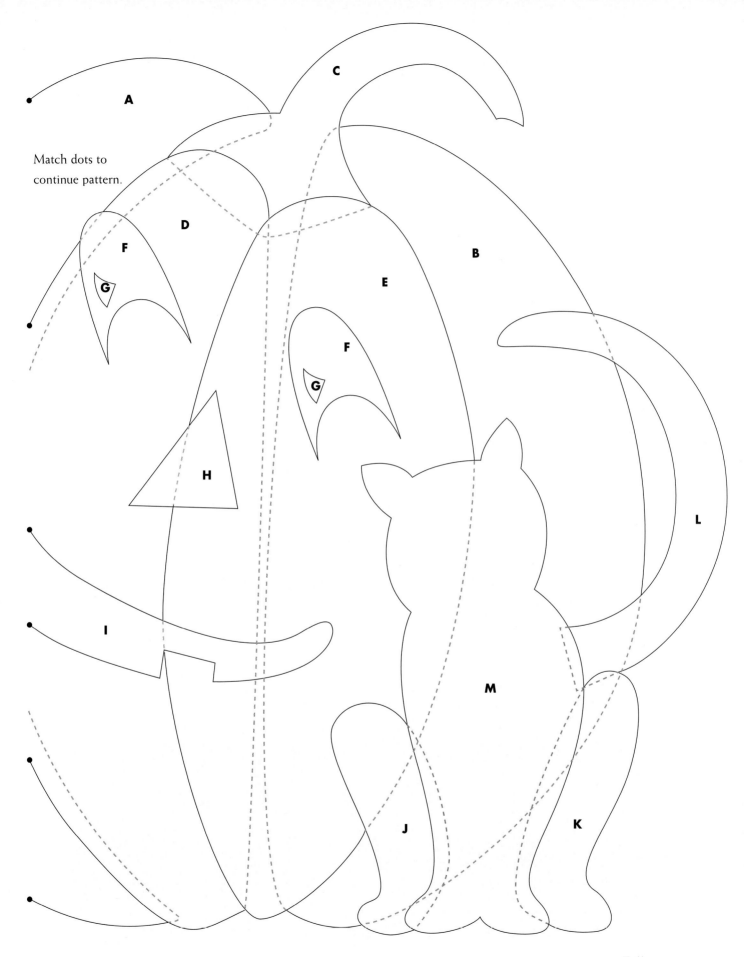

Match dots to
continue pattern.

A

C

D

F

G

E

B

F

G

H

L

I

M

J

K

Little Red Schoolhouse

Fall often triggers memories of starting school and meeting new friends. What better time to start a Schoolhouse quilt? This classic beauty has been around for many generations and maintains its timeless appeal.

Finished Size: 88½" x 88½"   Blocks: 9 (24") Schoolhouse Blocks

Quilt designed and made by Terry Clothier Thompson

materials

1½ yards tan-and-red print

4¼ yards red print

3 yards white

1½ yards solid red

8¼ yards fabric for backing and binding

Queen-size batting

Template material

cutting

Measurements for cutting include ¼" seam allowances. Cut all strips crosswise. Make templates for patterns C, D, E, and O.

From tan-and-red print, cut:

• 5 (9⅜"-wide) strips. Cut strips into 18 (9⅜") squares. Cut squares in half diagonally to make 36 setting triangles (X).

From red print, cut:

• 6 (13"-wide) strips. Cut strips into 18 (13") squares. Cut squares in half diagonally to make 36 setting triangles (Y).

• 9 (3½"-wide) strips for outer borders.

• 15 (2⅜"-wide) strips. Cut strips into 232 (2⅜") squares for pieced sashing.

From white, cut:

• 13 (4"-wide) strips. Cut strips into 122 (4") squares. Cut squares in quarters diagonally to make 488 triangles for pieced sashing.

• 3 (1¾"-wide) strips. From these:
   • Cut 9 (1¾" x 4¾") rectangles (B).
   • Cut 36 (1¾" x 2¼") rectangles (A).

• 1 (4¼"-wide) strips. Cut 9 Cs, using template on page 90.

• 4 (2¾"-wide) strips. From these:
   • Cut 9 Es and 9 Es rev., using template on page 91.

• Cut 9 (2¾" x 4½") rectangles (L).

• 4 (2¼"-wide) strips. From these:
   • Cut 9 (2¼" x 6½") rectangles (J).
   • Cut 9 (2¼" x 7½") rectangles (K).

From solid red, cut:

• 1 (1¾"-wide) strip. Cut strip into 18 (1¾" x 2¼") rectangles (A).

• 2 (4¼"-wide) strips. Cut 9 Ds, using template on page 91.

• 2 (1"-wide) strips. From these:
   • Cut 18 (1" x 2¼") rectangles (F).
   • Cut 9 (1" x 3½") rectangles (G).

• 2 (1⅝"-wide) strips. Cut strips into 18 (1⅝" x 4½") rectangles (H).

• 7 (1½"-wide) strips. From these:
   • Cut 18 (1½" x 5¾") rectangles (I).
   • Cut 9 (1½" x 2¾") rectangles (M).
   • Cut 18 (1½" x 5½") rectangles (N).

• 2 (4¾"-wide) strips. Cut 9 Os, using template on page 90.

assembly

Making Schoolhouse Blocks

1. Referring to *Block Assembly Diagram*, join 2 red As to each end of 1 B. Join 1 C to the left end of 1 D. Join A/B unit to C/D unit, matching seam. Set in E rev. to complete right side of roof unit.

2. Join 2 white As to 1 F as shown. Repeat to make 2 units. Join each unit to long sides of 1 G to make

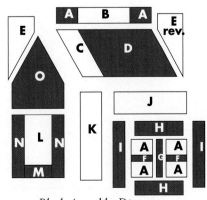

Block Assembly Diagram

window unit. Join 1 H to top and bottom of window unit. Add 1 I to each side. Join 1 J to top and 1 K to left side to complete house side.

3. Join 1 L and 1 M as shown. Add 1 N to each side. Join O to top of L/M/N unit. Add E to top left of O to complete door unit.

4. Join roof unit to house side unit. Set in door unit to complete block.

5. Referring to *Setting Diagram*, add 1 tan-and-red print triangle X to opposite sides of block. Add Xs to remaining 2 sides.

6. Referring to *Setting Diagram*, add 1 red print triangle Y to opposite sides of block. Add Ys to remaining 2 sides. Block should measure 24½" square, including seam allowance. Repeat to make 9 Schoolhouse Blocks.

making sashing and border strips

1. Join 2 white border triangles to opposite sides of each 2⅜" red print border square as shown in *Sashing Assembly Diagram* to make sashing units. Join 9 sashing units to make →

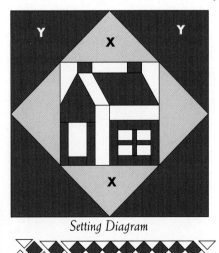

Setting Diagram

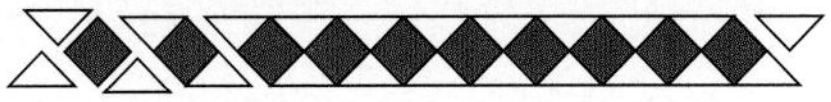

Sashing Assembly Diagram

sashing strip. Add extra white triangles to each end as shown. Repeat to make 6 sashing strips.

2. In a similar manner, join sashing units to make 4 (29-unit) border strips and 2 (31-unit) border strips. Add 1 triangle to each end of each strip as shown to complete border strips.

quilt assembly

1. Join 3 Schoolhouse Blocks with 2 (9-unit) sashing strips. Make 3 of these rows. Trim white triangles even with blocks.

2. Join 1 (29-unit) border strip to top of each block row. Join rows. Add 1 (29-unit) border strip to bottom block row. Trim white triangles as before.

3. Add 1 (31-unit) border strip to opposite sides of quilt.

4. Join 3½"-wide border strips into 1 long strip. Measure, trim, and add outer borders, mitering corners.

5. Cut 3 (2¾-yard) lengths of backing material. Join 3 panels lengthwise to make backing.

6. Layer backing, batting, and quilt top. Baste. Quilt as desired. Quilt

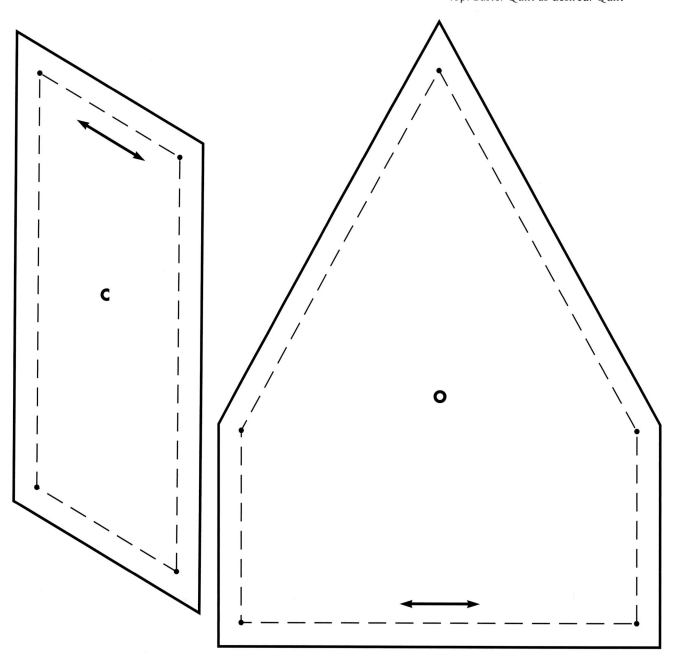

shown was quilted in-the-ditch around schoolhouses, grid-quilted in red setting triangles, and has triangles quilted in tan-and-red setting triangles. The sashing squares are echo-quilted, and there are alternating triangles quilted in red border.

7. Quilt has single-layer binding. Narrow strip of backing material is sewn to red print border, folded to back, and then handstitched in place. Cut 4 (1"-wide) lengthwise strips from excess backing material. Join ends with diagonal seams to make

10½ yards of binding. Fold under 1 edge ¼" and press. From front, sew raw edge of binding to edge of outer border with folded "flap" on top. Fold to back and slipstitch in place, mitering corners on back.

❖ *If you prefer, use additional red fabric to cut and bind quilt in the traditional manner.*
— Marianne

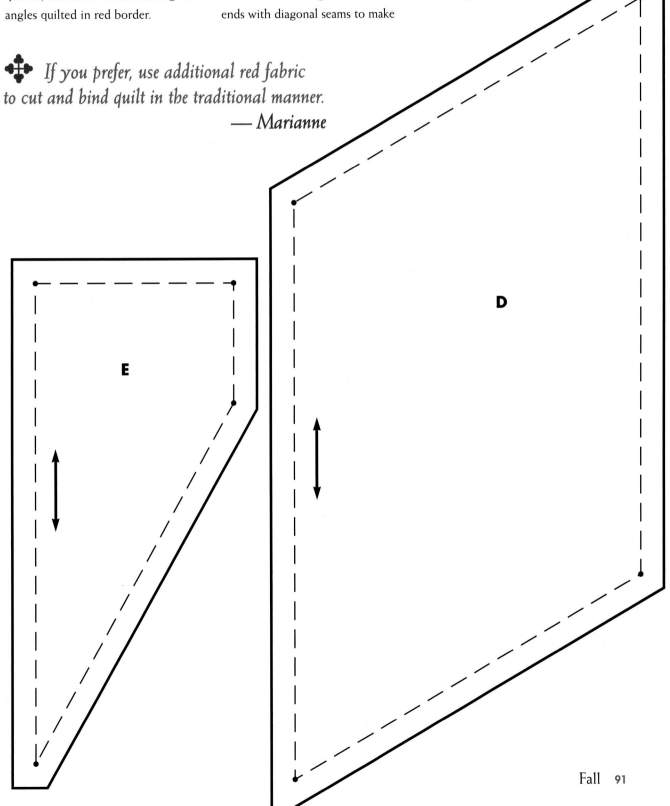

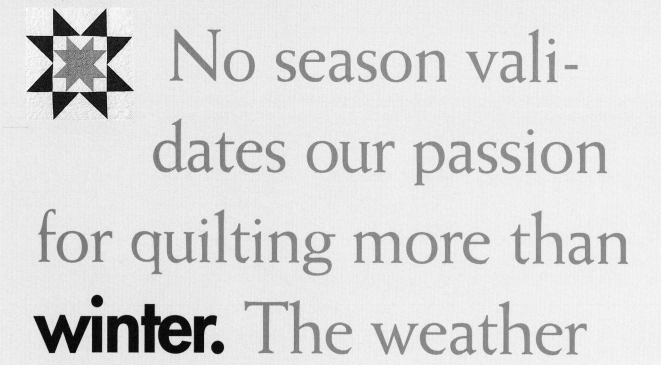 No season validates our passion for quilting more than **winter.** The weather

 can be bitter, but our hearts are **warm** whenever

we see our loved ones

snuggled under the soft, **thick** layers of one of our **quilts.** So as you stitch this January,  remember you are blanketing your family in **love.**

Double Sawtooth

Double Sawtooth is the ideal pattern to display a special collection of fat quarters. The large block centers showcase unique prints, and the points add an element of intricacy. In this setting, the blocks create four-patches where they meet.

Finished Size: 98¾" x 98¾"   Blocks: 61 (10") Double Sawtooth Blocks

materials

21 dark print fat quarters* (use more for variety)

13 light print fat quarters* (use more for variety)

4½ yards red print for setting triangles, border, and binding

9 yards fabric for backing

King-size batting

#96 Omnigrid® triangle ruler

*Fat quarter = 18" x 22"

cutting

Measurements include ¼" seam allowances. Border strips are exact length needed. You may want to cut them longer to allow for piecing variations.

Referring to Cutting Diagram, from each dark fat quarter, cut:

• 4 (2½" x 22") strips. Set aside 3 strips for use in triangle sets. Cut other strip into 6 (2½") squares (B).

• 1 (6½"-wide) strip. Cut strip into 3 (6½") squares (C).

From each light fat quarter, cut:

• 5 (2½" x 22") strips for cutting triangle sets.

• 2 (2½" x 22") strips. Cut strips into 122 (2½") squares (B) in sets of 2 to match triangle sets above.

From red print, cut:

• 3 yards. Cut 4 (7½"-wide) lengthwise strips for outer border. Cut strips into 2 (7½" x 85¼") side borders and 2 (7½" x 99¼") top and bottom borders.

• From remainder, cut 4 (2¼"-wide) lengthwise strips for binding.

• 3 (15½"-wide) crosswise strips. Cut strips into 5 (15½") squares. Cut squares in quarters diagonally to make 20 side setting triangles.

• 2 (8") squares. Cut squares in half diagonally to make 4 corner setting triangles.

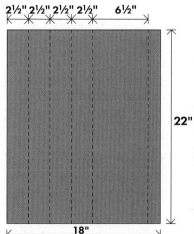

Cutting Diagram for Dark Fabrics

2½" 2½" 2½" 2½"   6½"

18"

22"

block assembly

1. Place 1 dark 2½"-wide strip atop 1 light 2½"-wide strip, right sides facing (*Photo A*). Using 2" marking on #96 Omnigrid ruler, cut triangle set (*Photo B*). Turn ruler and cut another set (*Photo C*). Continue in this manner to cut 12 A triangle sets. **Note:** If you do not plan to use this ruler, use Pattern A on page 96 to cut triangle sets. Keep sets together. ⟶

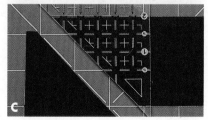

2. Choose 12 matching A triangle sets, 2 dark B and 2 light B squares to match, and 1 matching C square.

3. Stitch along long side of triangle sets. Press open to make 12 A triangle squares. Join into 4 strips of 3 triangle-squares as shown in *Block Assembly Diagram*.

4. Join 1 triangle square strip to opposite sides of 1 matching dark C square. Add 1 dark B and 1 light B to opposite ends of remaining triangle strips as shown. Add to top and bottom as shown to complete 1 Double Sawtooth Block *(Block Diagram)*.

5. Make 61 Double Sawtooth Blocks. If you prefer, mix point sets and center squares to create a few maverick blocks.

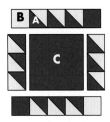

Block Assembly Diagram

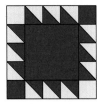

Block Diagram

quilt assembly

1. Arrange blocks and setting triangles as shown in *Quilt Top Assembly Diagram*. Join into diagonal rows; join rows to complete center.

2. Add red print side borders to quilt. Add top and bottom borders.

quilting and finishing

1. Divide backing fabric into 3 (3-yard) lengths. Join lengths to make backing.

2. Layer backing, batting, and quilt top; baste. Quilt as desired. Quilt shown was machine-quilted with trees in block centers and in borders. Setting triangles feature holly leaf.

3. Join 2¼"-wide red print strips into 1 continuous piece for straight-grain French-fold binding. Add binding to quilt.

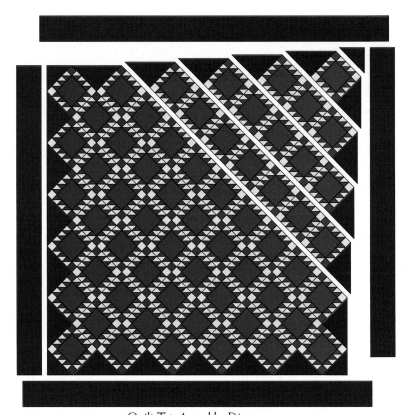

Quilt Top Assembly Diagram

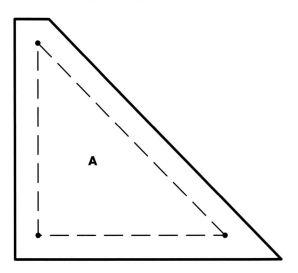

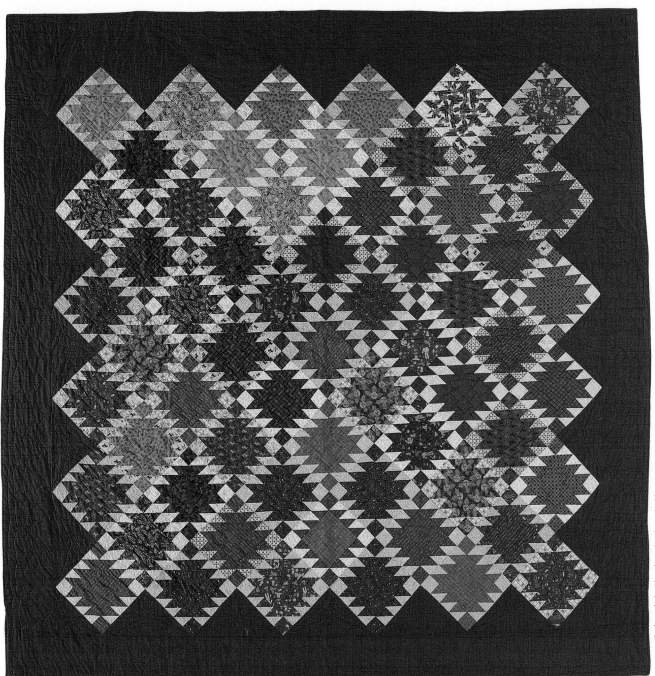

Quilt made by Rhonda Richards; quilted by New Traditions

Hoy's Tree Farm

Elsie Hoy and her husband began planting Christmas trees in 1981. After learning how to appliqué, Elsie knew she had to make a tree quilt. The result was Hoy's Tree Farm, which she made for her son, Mike, and his wife, Laura, whose own farm boasts more than 40,000 Christmas trees.

Finished Size: 84" x 96"   Blocks: 30 (12") Blocks

materials

15 fat quarters* red prints for blocks

14 fat quarters* cream prints for blocks

8 fat eighths** assorted green prints for trees

30 (4") squares assorted brown prints for tree trunks

6 fat eighths** black prints for pieced border

2 yards black pine-needle print for pieced borders (3½ yards for unpieced borders)

1¾ yards red print for pieced borders and binding (3½ yards for unpieced borders)

7½ yards fabric for backing

Queen-size batting

Paper-backed fusible web (optional)

Black embroidery floss

*Fat quarter = 18" x 22"

**Fat eighth = 9" x 22"

cutting

Measurements include ¼" seam allowances. Cut crosswise strips unless otherwise noted.

From each red fat quarter, cut:

- 7 (2½" x 22") strips. Cut strips into 56 (2½") squares (A) for total of 840 As.

From 13 cream fat quarters, cut from each:

- 3 (4½" x 22") strips. Cut strips into 12 (4½") squares (B). You will need 150 total. You will have 6 extra.
- 1 (2½" x 22") strip. Cut strip into 8 (2½") squares (A). You will have 104 total.

From 1 cream fat quarter, cut:

- 2 (2½" x 22") strips. Cut strips into 16 (2½") squares, to make total of 120 As.

From each green fat eighth, cut:

- 4 trees. You will have 2 extra.

From assorted brown prints, cut:

- 30 tree trunks.

From each black fat eighth, cut:

- 1 (4½" x 22") strip. Cut strip into 22 (4½") squares (border B).

From black pine-needle print, cut:

- 9 (3½"-wide) strips. Piece to make 2 (3½" x 87½") side borders and 2 (3½" x 81½") top and bottom borders. If you prefer unpieced borders, cut 2½ yards from alternate yardage. Cut 4 (3½"-wide) lengthwise strips and proceed.
- 3 (2½"-wide) strips. Cut strips into 48 (2½") squares (A).
- 8 (2½"-wide) strips. Cut strips into 22 (2½" x 12½") C rectangles.
- 1 (2½"-wide) strip. Cut strip into 4 (2½" x 4½") D rectangles.
- 1 (2½"-wide) strip. Cut strip into 4 (2½" x 6½") E rectangles.

From red print, cut:

- 17 (2"-wide) strips. Piece to make 2 (2" x 84½") inner side borders, 2 (2" x 75½") inner top and bottom borders, 2 (2" x 93½") outer side borders, and 2 (2" x 84½") outer top and bottom borders. If you prefer unpieced borders, cut 2¾ yards from alternate yardage. Cut 8 (2"-wide) strips lengthwise and proceed.
- 10 (2¼"-wide) strips for binding.

block assembly

1. Join 3 assorted red A squares and 1 cream A square to make 1 A unit (*Diagram 1*). Make 4 A units.

2. Using diagonal-seams method, lay 1 red A square atop left corner of 1 cream B square. Stitch diagonally and trim excess. Press open to reveal triangle. Repeat on adjacent side to make 1 A/B unit (*Diagram 2*). Make 4 A/B units.

3. Lay out 4 A units, 4 A/B units, and 1 cream B square as shown in *Block Assembly Diagram*. Join into rows; join rows to complete block (*Block Diagram*).

4. Appliqué 1 tree trunk and 1 tree to center of cream area, using blanket stitch.

5. Make 30 blocks. ⟶

Diagram 1

Diagram 2

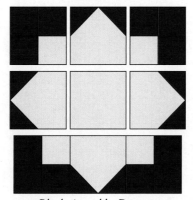

Block Assembly Diagram

Block Diagram

border assembly

1. Referring to *Border Unit Assembly Diagram*, join 3 assorted red A squares and 1 black print A square to make 1 A unit. Make 48 A units.

2. Using diagonal-seams method, join 1 red A square to 1 black print B square. Repeat on adjacent side to make 1 A/B unit. Make 22 A/B units.

3. Using diagonal-seams method and referring to *Border Unit Assembly Diagram*, join 1 red A square to each end of 1 C rectangle. Make 22 A/C units.

4. Join 2 A units, 1 A/B unit, and 1 A/C unit as shown in *Border Unit Diagram* to make 1 border unit. Make 22 border units.

5. Using diagonal-seams method and referring to *Border Corner Diagrams*, join 1 red A square to lower end of 1 D rectangle. Make 4 A/D units.

6. Using diagonal-seams method, join 1 red A square to right end of 1 E rectangle. Make 4 A/E units.

7. Join 1 A unit, 1 A/D unit, and 1 A/E unit as shown in *Border Corner Diagrams* to make 1 border corner unit. Make 4 border corner units.

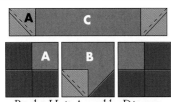

Border Unit Assembly Diagram

Border Unit Diagram

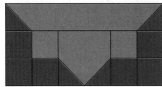

Border Corner Diagrams

quilt assembly

1. Lay out blocks in 6 horizontal rows of 5 blocks each. Join into rows; join rows to complete center.

2. Join 6 border units into strip as shown in *Quilt Top Assembly Diagram*. Repeat. Join to each side of quilt, matching seams.

3. Join 5 border units into strip. Add 1 corner unit to each end as shown. Repeat. Join to top and bottom of quilt, matching seams.

4. Measure length of quilt. Trim red inner borders to size and add to opposite sides of quilt top. Press seam allowance toward borders. Measure width of quilt, including borders. Trim remaining 2 borders to size. Join to top and bottom of quilt.

5. In same manner, add black borders to quilt. Add red outer borders to quilt.

quilting and finishing

1. Divide backing fabric into 3 (2½-yard) lengths. Join along long sides to make backing. Seams will run horizontally.

2. Layer backing, batting, and quilt top; baste. Quilt as desired. Quilt shown was quilted in-the-ditch around each red and cream area. Cream areas are filled with meander pattern, and red areas feature looped tree design. Borders have looped meander patterns mixed with stars.

3. Join 2¼"-wide red print strips into 1 continuous piece for straight-grain French-fold binding. Add binding to quilt.

Quilt Top Assembly Diagram

Tree

Trunk

Trace, scan, or
photocopy this
quilt label to
finish your quilt.

Quilt Label

Northwoods Cabin

Liz Porter combined lots of plaid, striped, checked, and print flannels to make this snuggly medallion quilt. It makes a beautiful Christmas quilt, but the outdoors theme is also great for decorating throughout the cold winter months.

Finished Size: 78" x 90"

materials

Note: All fabrics in quilt shown are 100% cotton flannel.

2 yards assorted dark greens for trees and borders

½ yard tan-and-red plaid for appliquéd tree backgrounds

2½ yards assorted light prints and plaids for background

½ yard assorted brown prints for tree trunks, appliqués, and borders

¼ yard each of 5 assorted blue plaids for small star centers, appliqués, and borders

¼ yard each of 5 assorted red plaids/stripes for small star points, appliqués, and borders

¼ yard each of 5 assorted tan-and-brown plaids for small star backgrounds, appliqué, and borders

⅛ yard each of 4 medium greens for appliquéd trees

⅞ yard red-green-navy-and-yellow plaid for large star points and borders

⅞ yard tan-and-black check for large star corner background

1 yards tan-and-black stripe for large star sides background

5½ yards yellow-and-green plaid for backing

1 yard assorted scraps for appliqués and pieced borders

¾ yard green print for binding

Double-size batting

Buttons: 4 white for fish bubbles,
    6 black for eyes and doorknobs,
    21 assorted for stars

#8 black pearl cotton

Template material

Note: Make all cuts in crosswise strips unless otherwise noted. Cutting instructions for Joseph's Coat borders

are exact length. You may cut extra strips from leftover fabrics for Joseph's Coat borders.

making center

From assorted dark greens, cut:
- 4 dark green trees, using appliqué pattern on page 105.

From tan-and-red plaid, cut:
- 1 (8½"-wide) strip. Cut strip into 4 (8½") squares for tree background.

From 5 assorted blue plaids, cut:
- 5 (4½") squares (A), 1 from each fabric.

From 5 assorted red plaids and stripes, cut:
- 5 sets of 8 (2½") squares (D), 1 set from each fabric.

From 5 assorted tan-and-brown plaids, cut:
- 5 sets of 4 (2½") squares (B) and 4 (2½" x 4½") rectangles (C), 1 set from each fabric.

1. Appliqué 1 tree to each red-and-tan 8½" square.

2. Join 1 D to each end of 1 C (*Star Diagonal Seams Diagrams*). Make 20 units.

3. Referring to *Star Block Assembly Diagram*, arrange C/D units, matching B squares, and 1 A square as shown. Join into horizontal rows; then join rows to complete block. Make 5 blocks.

4. Referring to photo and to *Quilt Top Assembly Diagram*, lay out 5 star blocks and 4 tree blocks. Join into rows; then join rows to complete center of large star. ⟶

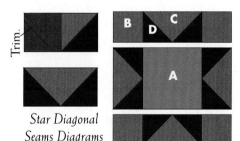

Star Diagonal Seams Diagrams

Star Block Assembly Diagram

Quilt Top Assembly Diagram

making large star

From red-green-navy-and-yellow plaid, cut:

- 2 (12⅞"-wide) strips. Cut strips into 4 (12⅞") squares. Cut squares in half diagonally to make 8 triangles (large star points).

From tan-and-black check, cut:

- 2 (12½"-wide) strips. Cut strips into 4 (12½") squares (large star corner appliqué backgrounds).

From tan-and-black stripe:

- 1 (25¼") squares. Cut squares in quarters diagonally to make 4 triangles.

1. Referring to photo and to materials list, cut out the following pieces as indicated, using patterns on pages 105–107. Appliqué in order given. Add buttons as shown. Note orientation of striped pieces in photo on page 102 as you appliqué.

Block 1 (upper left corner): 2 medium stars and 1 large star on tan-and-black check square.

Block 2 (top triangle): 1 moon, 2 small stars, and 1 medium star on tan-and-black stripe triangle.

Block 3 (upper right corner): 1 large star and 3 small stars on tan-and-black check square.

Block 4 (right side triangle): 1 bear, and 1 small star on tan-and-black stripe triangle.

Block 5 (lower right corner): 1 small star, 1 pond, and 1 canoe on tan-and-black check square.

Block 6 (bottom triangle): 3 fish and 3 fins on tan-and-black stripe triangle.

Block 7 (lower left corner): 1 house, 1 chimney, 1 roof, 1 door, and

1 window on tan-and-black check square.

Block 8 (left side triangle): 1 moose and 1 small star on tan-and-black stripe triangle.

2. Join 1 large star point to each short side of 1 triangle appliqué block to form a rectangle. Repeat for all 4 triangle appliqué blocks.

3. Lay out corner appliqué blocks, triangle appliqué units, and center assembly as shown in *Quilt Top Assembly Diagram* on page 103. Join into horizontal rows; then join rows to complete large star.

making tree border

From assorted dark greens, cut:

- 20 (2½"-wide) strips. Cut strips into:
  - 30 (2½" x 4½") Es.
  - 30 (2½" x 5½") Gs.
  - 30 (2½" x 6½") Is.
  - 30 (2½" x 7½") Ks.

From assorted light prints and plaids, cut:

- 27 (2½"-wide) strips. Cut strips into:
  - 60 (2½" x 4") Fs.
  - 120 (2½" x 3½") Hs and Ns.
  - 60 (2½" x 3") Js.
  - 60 (2½" x 2½") Ls.
- 4 (1½"-wide) strips. Cut strips into 17 (1½" x 7½") spacers.
- 2 (2"-wide) strips. Cut strips into 6 (2" x 7½") spacers.
- 1 (2½"-wide) strip. Cut strip into 5 (2½" x 7½") spacers.
- 3 (3½"-wide) strips. Cut strips into 12 (3½" x 7½") spacers.

From 1 brown print, cut:

- 2 (2½"-wide) strips. Cut strips into 30 (1½ " x 2½") rectangles for tree trunks (M).

1. Referring to *Tree Diagonal Seams Diagrams*, make Row 1 by placing 1 F perpendicular to 1 E. Stitch along diagonal and trim excess. Unfold and press. Repeat on other end of E with 1 F.

2. For Rows 2–4, repeat with 2 Hs and 1 G, 2 Js and 1 I, and 2 Ls and 1 K.

3. Join 1 N to each side of 1 M for Row 5. Join rows to complete block (*Tree Block Diagram*). Make 30 blocks.

4. Make 1 side border by alternating 6 (1½" x 7½") spacers and 5 blocks lengthwise. Repeat for second side border. Do not join to quilt yet.

5. Join spacers to tops and bottoms of remaining blocks as follows:

- 6 blocks with 3½" spacer at top.
- 6 blocks with 3½" spacer at bottom.
- 3 blocks with 1½" spacer at top and 2½" spacer at bottom.
- 2 blocks with 2½" spacer at top and 1½" spacer at bottom.
- 3 blocks with 2" spacers at top and bottom.

Tree Diagonal Seams Diagrams

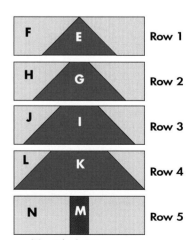

Tree Block Diagram

6. Referring to *Quilt Top Assembly Diagram* for placement, join 10 blocks together for top row. Repeat for bottom border. Do not join to quilt yet.

making joseph's coat border

1. Referring to *Joseph's Coat Strip Set Diagram,* join 5 to 7 strips into strip set measuring approximately 12" to 15" x 44". Make at least 5 strip sets.
2. Cut strip sets into 4½"-wide segments until set is used up.
3. Join segments end to end randomly to make borders. Inner borders should be approximately 4½" x 52½". Outer borders should be approximately 4½" x 74½" for top and bottom and 4½" x 86½" for quilt sides.

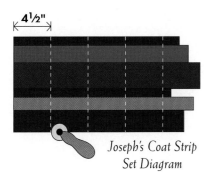

4½"

Joseph's Coat Strip Set Diagram

Note: Patterns do not include seam allowances.

❄ *To make this scrappy border, use mainly dark and red leftover fabric strips. Cut additional 1½"- to 3½"-wide strips as needed from leftover fabric. You will need approximately 1¾ yards for the borders.*
— *Liz*

Medium Star

Large Star

quilt top assembly

1. Starting on right side of large star, add 1 (4½" x 52½") striped border, in Log Cabin fashion, with bottom edge even with bottom of quilt (border will extend 4" beyond top edge of quilt). Leave top 7" of border unsewn as partial seam to be finished later. Add bottom border, left side border, and top border. Sew partial seam on first border.
2. Join tree side borders to quilt top. Add top and bottom tree borders. Cut 10 small stars from assorted fabrics and appliqué to tree borders. Add 1 button to center of each star.
3. Starting on left side, use partial seams to add 1 (4½" x 86½") striped border with bottom edge even with bottom of quilt (border will extend 4" beyond top edge of quilt). Add 1 (4½" x 74½") bottom border, 1 (4½" x 86½") right side border, and 1 (4½" x 74½") top border. Sew partial seam on first border.

Small Star

quilting and finishing

1. Divide backing fabric into 2 (2¾-yard) lengths. Cut 1 piece in half lengthwise. Sew 1 narrow panel to each side of wide panel. Press seam allowances toward narrow panel.
2. Layer backing, batting, and quilt top; baste. Quilt as desired. Quilt shown was utility-quilted, using size 8 black pearl cotton. Trees, borders, and large stars are quilted in-the-ditch, with 1 line of quilting going down center of each striped border. Appliqués have 2 rows of echo-quilting around each piece, with details, such as grass and waves, quilted in. There is loose star in house and canoe blocks. Center panel is grid-quilted through small stars and around trees.
3. For binding, cut 9 (2½"-wide) strips from green print. Make approximately 10 yards of French-fold straight-grain binding. Add binding to quilt.

→

Tree

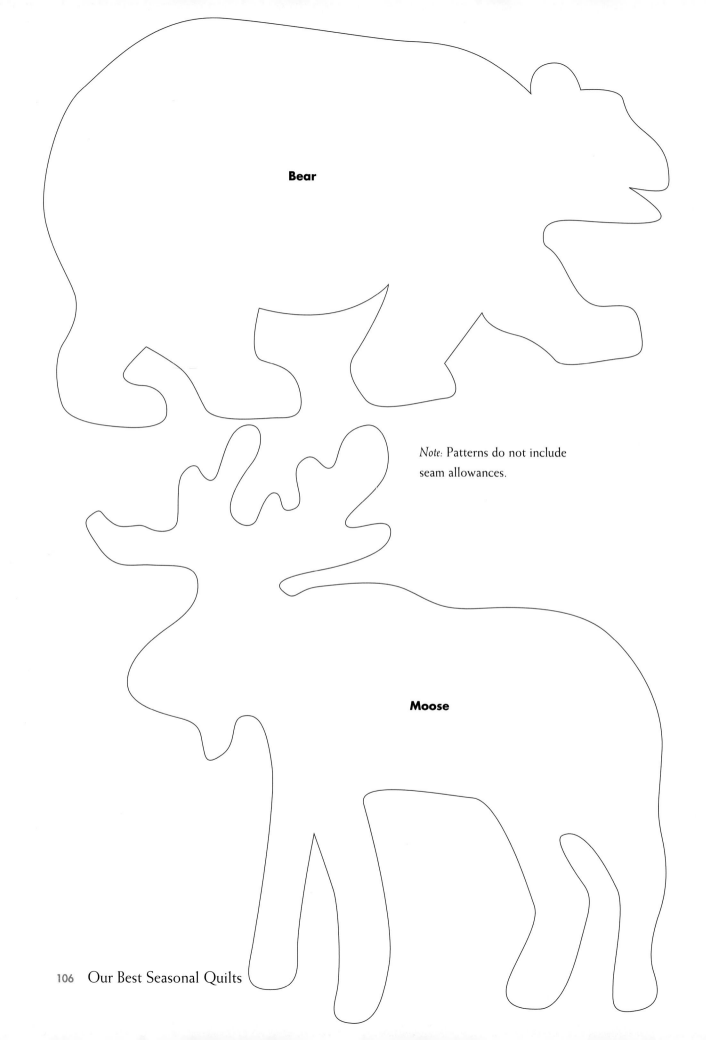

Bear

Note: Patterns do not include seam allowances.

Moose

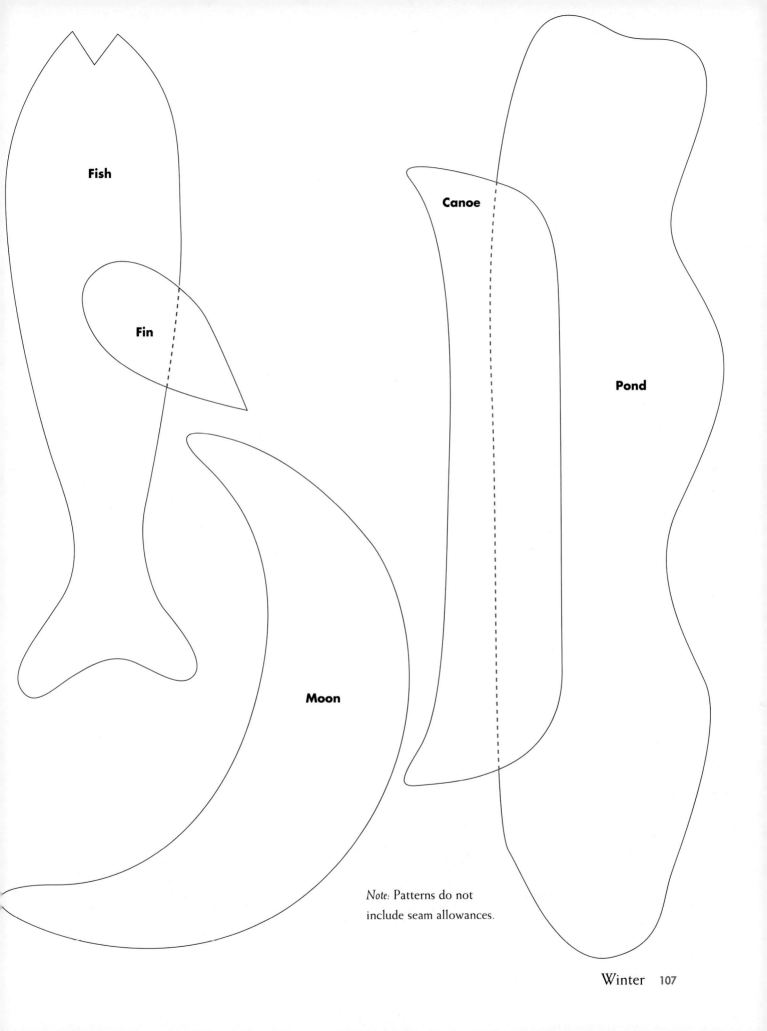

Fish

Fin

Canoe

Pond

Moon

Note: Patterns do not
include seam allowances.

Smoothing Iron Tree Skirt

The triangular Smoothing Iron blocks are similar in shape to the sole plate of an iron.
Learn to cut equilateral triangles as you make this skirt.

Finished Size: Approximately 49" in diameter
Blocks: 24 (12¼" high x 14" wide across base) triangular blocks (12 of each color variation)

Quilt designed and made by Liz Porter

Equilateral triangles, which have 3 (60°) angles, are basic to the Smoothing Iron Tree Skirt. Even if you, like many quilters, have little experience cutting equilateral triangles, the instructions on page 111 will make it easy to quick-cut all the pieces, using a rotary cutter and a ruler.

The Smoothing Iron Block name refers to the triangular flat iron sole plates that nineteenth-century women heated on stoves to press clothing. While most quilt blocks are square, Smoothing Iron is triangular.

materials

2 yards red-and-black check fabric
1½ yards white print fabric
1½ yards 54"- to 60"-wide muslin for
   backing
54" square batting
5 yards ¼"-diameter cable cord
Rotary cutter, acrylic ruler with
   guidelines for making cuts at
   60° angles, and cutting mat
Template material (optional)

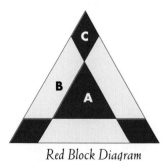

Red Block Diagram

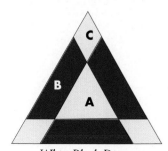

White Block Diagram

cutting

Measurements include ¼" seam allowances. Cut all strips crosswise.

From red and white fabrics, use instructions on page 111, "Cutting Smoothing Iron Pieces," to cut following from each:

- 2 (7¼"-wide) strips. From these, cut 12 A triangles.
- 9 (2½"-wide) strips. Cut 4 B wedges from each strip (total of 36 of each color).
- 3 (2½"-wide) strips. From these, cut total of 36 C diamonds.

From remaining red fabric, cut:

- 1 (1½"-wide) strip for ties.
- 5 yards of 1¼"-wide bias to cover cording. See "Making Continuous Bias Binding" (page 110) to make binding from 18" square.

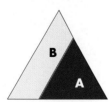

Diagram 1

Diagram 2

making blocks

Colors in red blocks and white blocks alternate to create tree skirt design (*Red Block Diagram* and *White Block Diagram*). Red block has red triangle and diamonds with white wedges. White block has white triangle and diamonds with red wedges.

1. To make red block, sew 1 white B wedge to 1 side of 1 red A triangle (*Diagram 1*). Press seam allowance toward B.

2. Referring to *Diagram 2*, sew 1 red C to 1 end of second white B. Press seam allowance toward C.

3. Join B/C unit to right-hand side of triangle unit (*Diagram 3*). Press seam allowance toward B.

4. Add red C to each end of third white B. Join C/B/C unit to bottom of triangle unit to complete block (*Diagram 4*). Press seam allowance toward B. Repeat steps to make 12 red blocks.

5. Repeat Steps 1–4 to make 12 white blocks, reversing colors as shown in *White Block Diagram*. ⟶

Diagram 3

Diagram 4

assembly

1. Sew 3 red blocks and 1 white block into large triangle as shown in *Triangle 1 Diagram*. Press seam allowances toward white blocks. Repeat to make 3 Triangle 1 blocks.

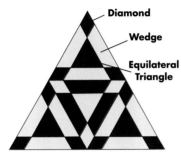

Triangle 1 Diagram

2. Sew 3 white blocks and 1 red block into large triangle as shown in *Triangle 2 Diagram*. Press seam allowances toward red blocks. Repeat to make 3 Triangle 2 blocks.

Triangle 2 Diagram

3. Trim 1" off top C diamond on each large triangle to make opening at center of tree skirt.

4. Join alternating large triangles into large hexagon as shown in photo on page 109, leaving 1 seam unsewn for side opening.

5. Cut red tie strip into 2 (22"-long) pieces. Turn under ¼" on both long edges and 1 short end of each strip; press. Fold each strip in half lengthwise, with wrong sides facing. Topstitch along all edges. Baste raw end of each strip to opposite corners at top of tree skirt opening.

quilting and finishing

1. Using zipper foot, cover cording with red continuous bias strips.

2. With raw edges aligned and using zipper foot, baste covered cording around outer edge of tree skirt.

3. Place batting on flat surface. Center muslin backing on top of batting. Center tree skirt right side down on top of muslin. Pin layers together.

4. Using zipper foot, sew layers together, leaving 1 side unsewn along tree skirt opening for turning. Trim excess batting and muslin, leaving ¼" seam allowances. Turn right side out through opening. Slipstitch opening closed.

5. Quilt as desired. Tree skirt shown has tree quilted in each A triangle (see *Quilting Pattern* below).

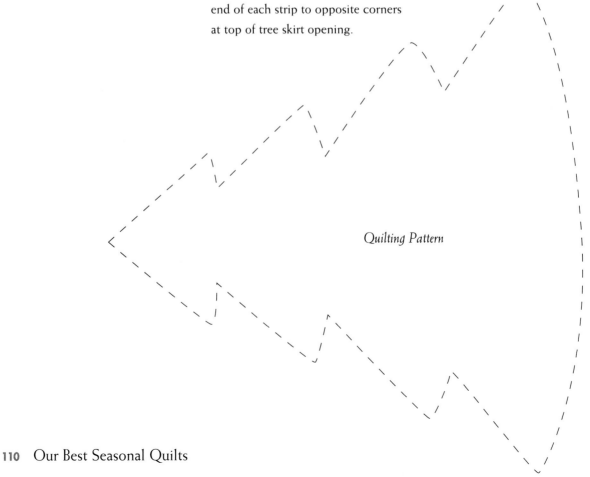

Quilting Pattern

cutting smoothing iron pieces

Using a ruler that has marks for 60° angles, it's easy to cut all the pieces you need for *Smoothing Iron Tree Skirt*.

To get the maximum number of pieces from each strip, open strips to full length and cut single layers.

Diamonds

1. Align ruler's 60° guide with 1 long edge of 2½"-wide strip. Cut along edge of ruler to trim end of strip at 60° angle. Discard end.

2. Position ruler parallel to and 2⅞" away from first 60° cut. Use rotary cutter to cut along edge of ruler.

3. Continue to make 60°-angle cuts spaced at 2⅞" intervals (*Diamond Diagram*). You should be able to cut approximately 14 diamonds from each strip.

To check cutting accuracy of diamonds, fold diamond in half to form an equilateral triangle. Points and all sides should match. — Liz

Equilateral Triangles

1. Referring to Step 1 of Diamonds, trim end of 7¼"-wide strip at 60° angle.

2. Pivot ruler to align 60° with strip's opposite long edge. Position ruler to cut triangle from strip. Cut along ruler's edge.

3. Continue pivoting ruler to cut strip into equilateral triangles (*Equilateral Triangle Diagram*). You should be able to cut approximately 8 or 9 triangles from each strip.

All three sides of equilateral triangles are the same size, and each of the three angles is 60°.

— Liz

Wedges

1. Referring to Step 1 of Diamonds, trim end of 2½"-wide strip at 60° angle.

2. Measure 7¾" along top of strip and mark.

3. Position ruler's 60° guide along top long edge of strip and ruler's edge at mark on fabric. Cut, referring to *Wedge Diagram* to be sure angle is in correct direction.

4. Measure 7¾" along bottom of strip and mark. Position ruler's 60° guide along bottom edge of strip and ruler's edge at mark on fabric. Cut, making sure that angle goes in opposite direction from previous cut (*Wedge Diagram*).

5. In same manner, cut 4 wedges from each strip.

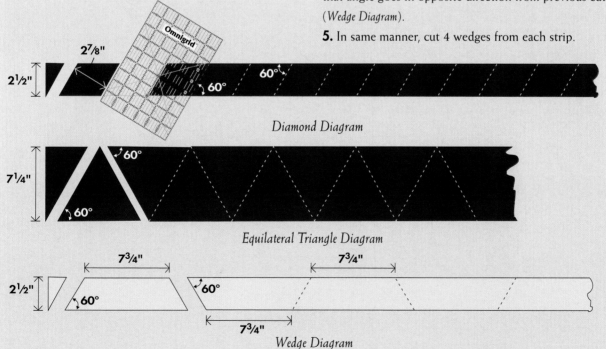

Diamond Diagram

Equilateral Triangle Diagram

Wedge Diagram

Christmas Laurel Leaves

By using red and green fabrics to sew the traditional Laurel Leaf appliqués on this quilt, you create an heirloom with a Christmas look.

Finished Size: 56½" x 72"   Blocks: 12 (15½") Blocks

materials

4¼ yards 90"-wide muslin for block background squares, borders, binding, and backing*

2 yards solid green fabric for appliqués

1 yard solid red fabric for appliqués

Twin-size batting

Thread to match fabrics

Template material

*To make the block background squares, 90"-wide muslin will give you the most efficient fabric use. If you use 45"-wide muslin, buy a total of 9¼ yards.

cutting

Refer to *Cutting Diagram* to cut muslin.

From 90"-wide muslin, cut:

- 1 (2-yard) length; from this, cut:
  - 4 (5½" x 65") lengthwise border strips.
  - 12 (16") background blocks.
  - 5 (2¼" x 64") strips for straight-grain binding.

Set aside remaining fabric for backing.

From green fabric, cut:

- 12 (⅞"-wide) crosswise stem strips.
- 316 leaves, using template.

From red fabric, cut:

- 200 leaves, using template.

assembly

Making Appliqué Blocks

Refer to *Block Diagram* throughout. Match thread color to appliqué fabric.

1. Fold background blocks in half diagonally in both directions. Press lightly to make placement lines.

2. With wrong sides facing, fold each green strip in half lengthwise. Stitch along long edges to make 12 tubes. Cut tubes into 16"-long segments for stems. Press so that seam falls on center of wrong side.

3. Baste 2 green stems into X along placement lines in center of background block and appliqué.

4. Appliqué red and green leaves around stem edges as shown. Space leaf points about 1" apart along stem.

Making Quilt Top

Refer to *Quilt Assembly Diagram* on page 114 throughout.

1. Join appliqué blocks in 4 horizontal rows of 3 blocks each, using white thread.

2. Trim 2 borders to 62½" long; sew to quilt sides. Trim 2 borders to 57" long and sew to quilt top and bottom.

3. Appliqué leaves to borders as shown. Position green leaf points at block seam lines and at center of white space in each block.

quilting and finishing

1. Layer backing, batting, and quilt top, with 90"-wide muslin selvages at top and bottom; baste. Quilt as desired.

2. Join muslin binding strips into 1 continuous 7½-yard long strip of straight-grain binding; add to quilt. →

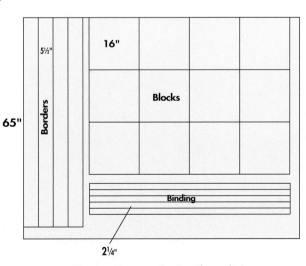

Cutting Diagram (90"-wide muslin)

Block Diagram

Quilt Assembly Diagram

Plaid Tidings

"I love appliqué designs," says Liz Porter, "but I don't have the patience or the time at this stage of my life to do them by hand. Besides, I really enjoy sewing on the machine. Fusible web and machine blanket stitching made this appliqué quilt go together quickly."

Finished Size: 86" x 112"
Blocks: 18 (16") Rose appliqué blocks, 10 side setting triangle appliqué blocks, 4 corner triangles

materials

6½ yard tan plaid for appliqué
  background

⅓ yard each of 9 assorted red prints
  and plaids for roses, center circles,
  sashing squares, and border
  triangles

Fat eighths* each of 9 assorted green
  prints and plaids for leaves and
  stems

6" squares each of 9 assorted gold prints
  and plaids for roses
  (¼ yard total)

3¼ yards green stripe for borders and
  sashing

1½ yards red print for borders, border
  corners, and binding

7½ yards fabric for backing

King-size batting

8 yards paper-backed fusible web
  (optional)

Gold machine embroidery thread or
  embroidery floss

*Fat eighth = 9" x 22"

cutting

Measurements include ¼" seam
allowance. Cut crosswise strips unless
otherwise noted. Border strips are
exact length needed; you may want
to make them longer to allow for
piecing variations. Follow manufacturer's instructions for fusing.

From tan plaid, cut:

• 9 (17"-wide) strips. Cut strips into
  18 (17") squares for appliqué background blocks. (Blocks will be
  trimmed to 16½" after appliqué is
  completed.)

• 3 (23⅞"-wide) strips. Cut strips into
  3 (23⅞") squares. Cut squares in
  quarters diagonally to make
  10 quarter-square triangles for side

triangle backgrounds. You will have
2 extra.

• From remainder, cut 2 (12¼")
  squares. Cut squares in half diagonally to make 4 half-square triangles
  for corner triangles.

From assorted red prints, cut:

• 18 matched sets of 4 Es and 1B for
  rose blocks, using templates on pages
  118 and 119.

• 10 assorted Es side triangles.

• 28 (4⅞") squares. Cut squares in half
  diagonally to make 56 half-square
  triangles for border appliqué (G).

• 31 (2½") sashing squares.

From assorted green prints, cut:

• 18 matched sets of the following
  for blocks:
  • 1 A, 4 Cs, and 4 Fs.

• 10 matched sets of the following
  for side triangles:
  • 1 C (short), and 1 F.

From assorted gold prints, cut:

• 18 matched sets of:
  • 4 Ds for blocks

• 10 assorted Ds for side triangles.

From green stripe, cut:

• 18 (2½"-wide) border strips.

• 24 (2½"-wide) strips. Cut strips
  into 48 (2½" x 16½") rectangles for
  sashing.

From red print, cut:

• 9 (1½"-wide) border strips.

• 11 (2¼"-wide) strips for binding.

• 1 (5½"-wide) strip. Cut strip into
  4 (5½") squares for border corners.

block assembly

1. Fold 1 (17") plaid square in quarters diagonally to make guide lines.

2. Referring to *Appliqué Placement
Diagram*, position A and B. Tuck stem
C under B. Tuck flower D and E and

leaf F under C. Fuse.

3. Machine- or hand-appliqué with
gold thread, using blanket-stitch (see
Blanket-Stitch Diagram on page 119).

4. Make 18 Rose appliqué blocks.
Trim to 16½".

Appliqué Placement Diagram

side triangle assembly

1. Fold 1 side triangle appliqué background in half to make guidelines.
Add 4 assorted Gs to outer long edge
of 1 side setting triangle and machine-
or hand-appliqué with gold thread,
using blanket-stitch. Do not blanket-
stitch edges that will be joined to
sashing. Baste along outer edge to
hold in position.

2. Referring to *Side Triangle Appliqué
Diagram*, position C–F. Fuse.
Machine- or hand-appliqué with
gold thread, using blanket-stitch.

3. Make 10 side setting triangle
appliquéd blocks.

Side Triangle Appliqué Diagram

corner triangle assembly

1. Referring to *Corner Triangle Diagram*, add 4 assorted Gs to outer edge of 1 corner triangle and machine-appliqué in place, using buttonhole stitch.

2. Make 4 corner triangles.

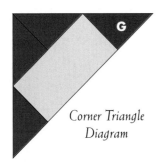

Corner Triangle Diagram

quilt top assembly

1. Referring to *Quilt Top Assembly Diagram*, lay out completed blocks, side triangles, and corner triangles in diagonal rows as shown. Alternate blocks and side triangles with green sashing strips and join into rows.

2. Referring to *Quilt Top Assembly Diagram*, alternate green sashing strips with 2½" red sashing squares and join end to end into sashing rows.

3. Alternate sashing rows and block rows and join in diagonal rows, matching seams. Add corner triangles to complete. Trim sashing squares at outer edge of quilt even with quilt sides so that they become triangles.

4. Join green border strips to make 4 (110"-long) and 4 (88"-long) strips. Join red border strips to make 2 (110"-long) and 2 (88"-long) strips. Join 1 green border to both sides of each red border.

5. Measure quilt length (approximately 102") and trim 2 borders to this length for quilt sides. Measure quilt width (approximately 76½") and trim 2 borders to this length for top and bottom borders.

6. Add 1 green and red side border to each side of quilt. Add 1 red 5½" square to each end of top and bottom borders. Add green and red top and bottom borders to quilt, matching seams.

quilting and finishing

1. Divide backing fabric into 3 (2½"-yard) lengths. Join along sides to make backing. Seams will be parallel to top and bottom of quilt.

2. Layer backing, batting, and quilt top; baste. Quilt as desired. Quilt shown was machine-appliquéd and machine-quilted. Each block is quilted in-the-ditch around edge and filled with outline quilting. Red triangles are outlined-quilted ¾" in from embroidery. Red border is quilted in-the-ditch, and quilting extends into corners to make cross pattern. Green sashing and borders have wave pattern.

3. Join 2¼"-wide red print strips into 1 continuous piece for straight-grain. French-fold binding. Add binding to quilt. ⟶

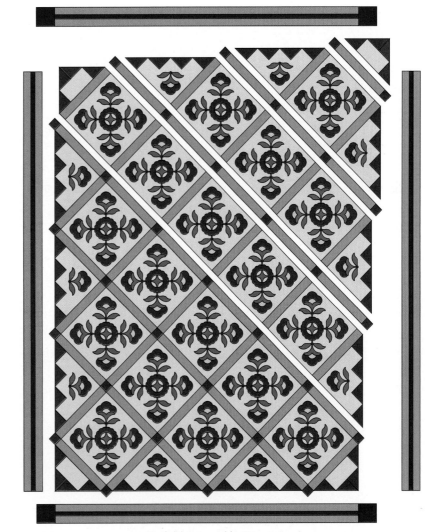

Quilt Top Assembly Diagram

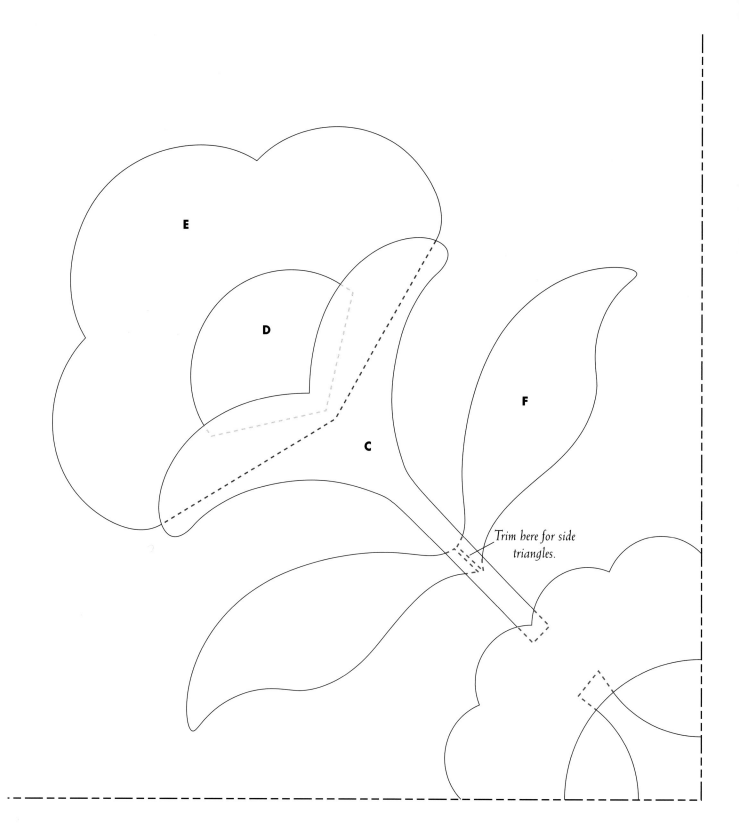

E

D

C

F

Trim here for side triangles.

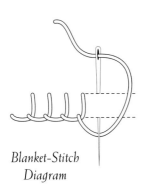

Blanket-Stitch Diagram

Quilt designed and made by Liz Porter; quilted by Lynn Witzenburg

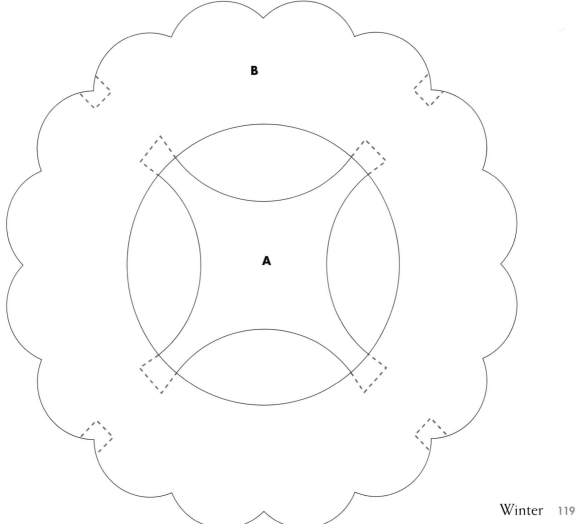

B

A

Winter   119

Starlight, Starbright

If you want a quilt that works well both during the holidays and the rest of the year, mix traditional reds and greens with golds, purples, and yellows, as in the quilt below. Change the red border to a black one, as shown on page 123, and the quilt takes on a Mardi Gras flair. Instructions for making the red quilt follow, but see "Two at a Time" (page 123) for timesaving tips to double your quilts.

Finished Size: 80" x 88" Large star blocks: 9 (16") Small star blocks: 36 (8")

materials

½ yard gold print

¾ yard yellow print

1 yard purple print

¾ yard green print

¾ yard red metallic print

2½ yards red angel print for blocks, outer border, and binding

4 yards white-on-white snowflake print for background and borders

2¼ yards black-and-white checkerboard print for border (½ yard for pieced border)

5½ yards white for backing

Full-size batting

cutting

Measurements include ¼" seam allowance. Unless otherwise noted, cut crosswise strips.

From gold print, cut:

- 1 (4½"-wide) strip. Cut strip into 5 (4½") squares (C).
- 2 (2⅞"-wide) strips. Cut strips into 20 (2⅞") squares. Cut squares in half diagonally to make 40 half-square triangles (A).

From yellow print, cut:

- 1 (4½"-wide) strip. Cut strip into 9 (4½") squares (C).
- 1 (4⅞"-wide) strip. Cut strip into 8 (4⅞") squares. Cut squares in half diagonally to make 16 half-square triangles (E).
- 3 (2⅞"-wide) strips. Cut strips into 36 (2⅞"-wide) squares. Cut squares in half diagonally to make 72 half-square triangles (A).

From purple print, cut:

- 2 (4⅞"-wide) strips. Cut strips into 12 (4⅞") squares. Cut squares in half diagonally to make 24 half-square triangles for (E).

- 2 (4½"-wide) strips. Cut strips into 10 (4½") squares (C).
- 3 (2⅞"-wide) strips. Cut strips into 40 (2⅞") squares. Cut squares in half diagonally to make 80 half-square triangles (A).

From green print, cut:

- 1 (4⅞"-wide) strip. Cut strip into 8 (4⅞") squares. Cut squares in half diagonally to make 16 half-square triangles (E).
- 1 (4½"-wide) strip. Cut strip into 9 (4½") squares (C).
- 3 (2⅞"-wide) strips. Cut strips into 36 (2⅞") squares. Cut squares in half diagonally to make 72 half-square triangles (A).

From red metallic print, cut:

- 1 (4⅞"-wide) strip. Cut strip into 8 (4⅞") squares. Cut squares in half diagonally to make 16 half-square triangles (E).
- 2 (4½"-wide) strips. Cut strips into 10 (4½") squares (C).
- 3 (2⅞"-wide) strips. Cut strips into 40 (2⅞") squares. Cut squares in half diagonally to make 80 half-square triangles (A).

From red angel print, cut:

- 4 (6½"-wide) lengthwise strips for borders.
- 1 (4½"-wide) crosswise strip. Cut strip into 2 (4½") squares, centering angel in square (C).
- 2 (2⅞"-wide) crosswise strips. Cut strips into 8 (2⅞") squares. Cut squares in half diagonally to make 16 half-square triangles (A). Set aside remainder for binding.

From white-on-white snowflake print, cut:

- 2¼ yards. From this, cut:
  - 4 (1½"-wide) lengthwise strips

for borders.

- 13 (2½"-wide) strips. Cut strips into 180 (2½") squares (D).
- 7 (5¼"-wide) strips. Cut strips into 45 (5¼") squares. Cut squares in quarters diagonally to make 180 quarter-square triangles (B).
- 4 (4½"-wide) strips. Cut strips into 36 (4½") squares (G).
- 3 (9¼"-wide) strips. Cut strips into 9 (9¼") squares. Cut squares in quarters diagonally to make 36 quarter-square triangles (F).

From checkerboard print, cut:

- 4 (1½"-wide) lengthwise strips for borders. If working with ½ yard, cut 8 (1½"-wide) crosswise strips and piece as needed to make borders.

making blocks

Making Small Sawtooth Stars

1. Join 1 (2⅞") colored A triangle to each short side of 1 (5¼") white B triangle to make a Goose Chase Unit (*Goose Chase Unit Diagram*). Make 4 matching Goose Chase units.

2. Referring to *Small Sawtooth Star Block Assembly Diagram*, lay out 4 Goose Chase units, 1 (4½") matching C square, and 4 (2½") white D squares as shown. Join into rows, pressing seam allowances toward squares. Then join rows to complete block (*Small Sawtooth Star Block Diagram*). ⟶

Goose Chase Unit Diagram

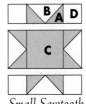

Small Sawtooth Star Block Assembly Diagram

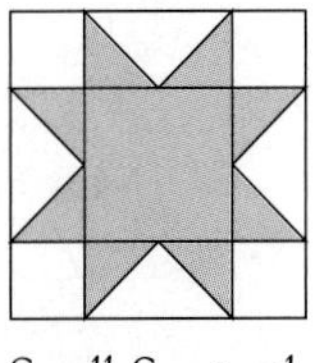

Small Sawtooth Star Block Diagram

3. Repeat Steps 1 and 2 to make 10 purple stars, 9 green stars, 9 yellow stars, 5 gold stars, 10 red metallic stars, and 2 red angel print stars, for total of 45 blocks.

Making Large Sawtooth Stars

1. Join 1 (4⅞") colored E triangle to each short side of 1 (9¼") white F triangle to make a large Goose Chase unit. Make 4 matching Goose Chase units.

2. Referring to *Large Sawtooth Star Block Assembly Diagram*, lay out 1 Small Sawtooth Star with 4 large Goose Chase units and 4 (4½") white G squares as shown. Join into rows; then join rows to complete block (*Large Sawtooth Star Block Diagram*).

3. Repeat Steps 1 and 2 to make 9 Large Stars, referring to photo as a color guide or mix colors as desired.

Quilt shown has 1 purple/gold star, 2 purple/yellow stars, 2 green/yellow stars, 2 red/red stars, 1 yellow/purple star, and 1 yellow/green star.

quilt assembly

1. Lay out blocks as shown in *Quilt Top Assembly Diagram*.

2. Working left to right and top to bottom, join adjacent small stars into strips. Add large stars as shown to make larger units.

3. Join Units 1–4 and Units 5–7; then join halves to complete inner quilt top.

4. Measure length of quilt, measuring through middle. Cut 2 white borders this length. Sew borders to 2 opposite sides of quilt. Press seam allowances toward borders. Measure width of quilt, including borders. Cut 2 white borders this length. Sew to quilt top and bottom. Press seam

allowances toward borders. Add checkerboard and red borders in same manner.

quilting and finishing

1. For backing, divide fabric into 2 (2¾-yard) lengths. Cut 1 piece in half lengthwise and join each panel to remaining full-width length. Press seam allowances toward narrow panels.

2. Layer backing, batting, and quilt top. Baste. Quilt as desired. Quilt shown is machine-quilted with stipple quilting in white areas. Star centers have snowflake motif in matching thread. Borders are quilted with angel design.

3. To make binding, cut 22 (2¼"-wide) strips from leftover angel fabric. Make 9¾ yards of French-fold straight-grain binding. Add binding to quilt.

Large Sawtooth Star Block Assembly Diagram

Large Sawtooth Star Block Diagram

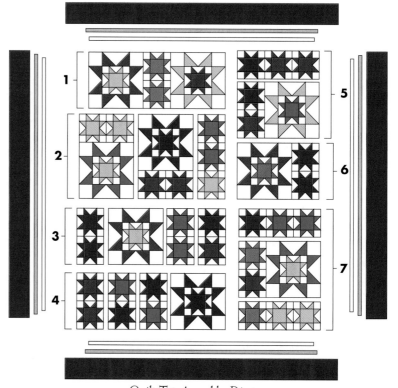

Quilt Top Assembly Diagram

two at a time

materials

When working with a strong theme fabric, such as the angel print shown below left, match tone-on-tone prints to it. While the fabrics used in these quilts read as solids from a distance, they are actually polka dots, metallic designs, and viney prints.

2½ to 3 yards theme print for each quilt for borders and binding

1 yard each of assorted colors to match border print (Quilts shown use red, green, gold, yellow, and purple.)

7 to 8 yards white background print

cutting

From each yard of colored fabric, cut:

• 2 (4⅞"-wide) strips. Cut strips into 4⅞" squares. Cut squares in half diagonally (E).

• 2 (4½"-wide) strips. Cut strips into 4½" squares (G).

• 5 (2⅞"-wide) strips. Cut strips into 2⅞" squares. Cut squares in half diagonally (A).

For added visual interest, make small stars from the theme fabric.

Follow instructions on page 121 for cutting white background fabric. Cut additional strips as needed to make 2 quilts.

Outer borders on both quilts were cut 6½" wide, to finish 6". Checkerboard borders were cut 1½" wide, to finish 1". You may adjust border widths to accommodate your bed size.

Quilts made by Rhonda Richards; machine-quilted by New Traditions

The finished size depends on the block arrangement. The red quilt measures 80" x 88", the black quilt measures 74" x 90". Another alternative is to make one bed-sized quilt and two wall hangings.

Mini Churn Dash

This tiny quilt makes a charming accent piece in almost any nook. Use it as a table-topper or hang it on a wall that needs a little color.

Finished Size: 12½" x 16¾" Blocks: 6 (3") Churn Dash Blocks

materials

Assorted scraps (at least 2" x 5") of
   12 dark prints

Fat eighth* light print

Fat eighth* blue print

½ yard red print

Fat quarter** fabric for backing

18" x 22" scrap batting

*Fat eighth = 9" x 22"

**Fat quarter = 18" x 22"

cutting

Measurements include ¼" seam allowances. Cut crosswise strips unless otherwise noted.

From assorted dark prints, cut:

• 6 sets of triangles. For each set, cut 2 matching (1⅞") squares. Cut squares in half diagonally to make 4 half-square triangles (A).

• 6 sets of rectangles. For each set, cut 4 matching (1" x 1½") rectangles (B).

From light print, cut:

• 2 (1½" x 22") strips. Cut strips into 6 (1½") squares (C) and 24 (1" x 1½") rectangles (B).

• 2 (1⅞" x 22") strips. Cut strips into 12 (1⅞") squares. Cut squares in half diagonally to make 24 half-square triangles (A).

From blue print, cut:

• 4 (¾" x 22") strips for inner border.

From red print, cut:

- 1 (5½"-wide) strip. Cut strip into:
  - 2 (5½") squares. Cut squares in quarters diagonally to make 8 quarter-square triangles for side setting triangles. You will have 2 extra.
  - 2 (3") squares. Cut squares in half diagonally to make 4 half-square triangles for corner setting triangles.
- 2 (3½") squares for setting blocks.
- 2 (2¼"-wide) strips for outer border.
- 2 (2¼"-wide) strips for binding.

block assembly

1. Join 1 dark A to 1 light A (*Unit A Diagram*). Make 4 matching A segments.

2. Join 1 dark B to 1 light B (*Unit B Diagram*). Make 4 matching B segments.

3. Arrange 1 C, 4 Unit As and 4 Unit Bs as shown in *Block Assembly Diagram*. Join into rows; join rows to complete block (*Block Diagram*).

4. Make 6 Churn Dash Blocks.

Unit A Diagram   *Unit B Diagram*

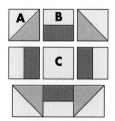

Block Assembly Diagram

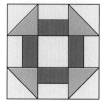

Block Diagram

quilt assembly

1. Arrange blocks, setting blocks, and setting triangles as shown in *Quilt Top Assembly Diagram*. Join in diagonal rows; join rows to complete quilt center.

2. Measure length of quilt. Trim blue borders to size (approximately 13¼")

Quilt Top Assembly Diagram

and add to opposite sides of quilt top. Press seam allowance toward borders. Measure width of quilt, including borders. Trim remaining 2 borders to size (approximately 9½"). Join to top and bottom of quilt.

3. Measure, trim, and add red border to quilt in the same fashion. Sides are approximately 13¾"; top and bottom are approximately 13".

quilting and finishing

1. Layer backing, batting, and quilt top; baste. Quilt as desired. Quilt shown was machine-quilted in-the-ditch around blocks and blue border.

2. Join 2¼"-wide red strips into 1 continuous piece for straight-grain French-fold binding. Add binding to quilt.　　　⟶

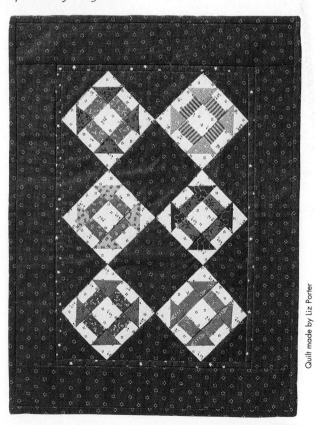

Quilt made by Liz Porter

Winter on the Ohio

Liz Porter purchased this small quilt at a silent auction held at the first Baltimore Appliqué Society Show in October 1996. For intricate patterns like this one, try freezer paper appliqué. You'll find instructions for how to do this appliqué method on page 128.

Finished Size: 21" x 21"

materials

¾ yard white-on-cream print for back-
    ground and binding
½ yard blue variegated print for
    center snowflake
½ yard blue snowflake print for
    borders
¾ yard muslin for backing
22" square batting
¾ yard 18"-wide freezer paper

cutting

From white-on-cream print, cut:
• 1 (22") square for background.

• 5 (2¼" x 22") strips for straight-grain
    binding.

From blue variegated print, cut:
• 1 (13") square for snowflake.

From blue snowflake print, cut:
• 4 (5" x 22") strips for borders.

From muslin, cut:
• 1 (22") square for backing.

assembly

1. Cut 1 (13") square of freezer
paper. Fold square into fourths and
crease to make guidelines. Trace ¼
snowflake pattern onto each section

of freezer paper, aligning fold lines
to make complete pattern. Cut out
pattern. Center and press freezer
paper right side of blue variegated
print. Cut out pattern roughly. With
freezer paper on top as guide,
appliqué snowflake onto 22" cream
background. (**Note:** See page 128 for
freezer paper appliqué instructions.)
2. Layer 2 (5" x 22") blue snowflake
print strips, with right sides facing.
Mark 45° angle at end, as shown in
Diagram 1 on page 128. Stitch over
along drawn line. Trim, unfold, and ⟶

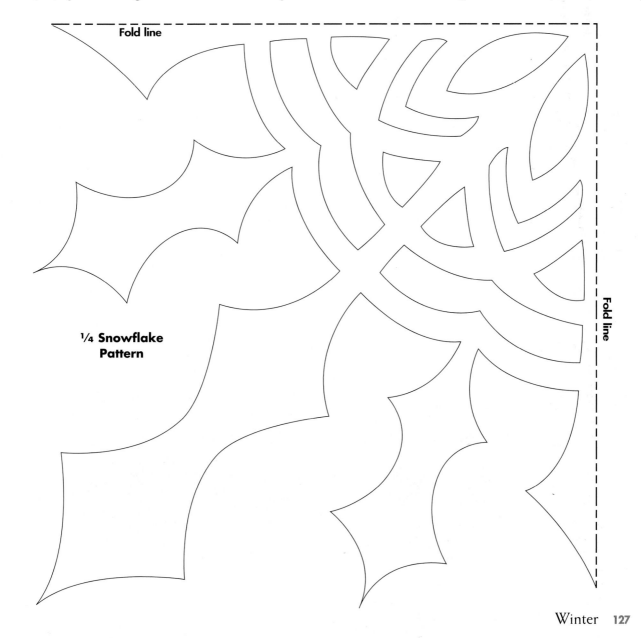

Fold line

**¼ Snowflake
Pattern**

Fold line

press to reveal mitered corner (*Diagram 2*). Repeat with remaining 2 strips.

3. To join 2 sections from Step 2, repeat for remaining corners, as shown in *Diagram 3*. Trim, unfold, and press to reveal border frame (*Diagram 4*).

4. Cut 4 (3" x 18") strips of freezer paper. Trace border pattern on opposite page onto 2 strips. Reverse pattern and trace onto 2 remaining strips.

Cut out pattern strips. Place each strip on right side of border frame, aligning outer edges and mitered seam lines. Press pattern onto fabric. Cut along inner border edge roughly. Center border frame over quilt center, with outer edges aligned, and pin in place. Appliqué border waves in same manner as snowflake.

quilting and finishing

1. Layer backing, batting, and quilt top. Baste. Quilt as desired. Quilt shown was outline-quilted around all appliqué and has echo-quilted scallop pattern in border.

2. From cream print, make 100" of straight-grain binding. Add binding to quilt.

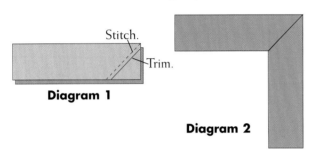

Diagram 1

Stitch.

Trim.

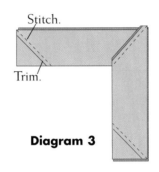

Diagram 2

Stitch.

Trim.

Diagram 3

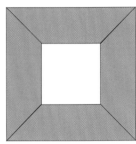

Diagram 4

needle-turn freezer-paper appliqué

1. Cut piece of freezer paper to size of appliqué and fold in half twice to form equal quadrants. Open, with coated side down, and trace ¼ of pattern on 1 section, aligning center and folds.

2. Refold paper. Place pins through pattern to keep folds aligned. Cut out; do not cut along fold lines.

3. Fold square of appliqué fabrics in half twice to form equal quadrants and press to form guidelines. Open freezer-paper pattern and position on right side of fabric, coated side down, aligning centers and folds. Using dry iron set for wool, press pattern onto fabric.

4. Position appliqué fabric on top of background fabric, with right sides facing up, and pin.

5. Start at any section of design and carefully cut

appliqué fabric approximately ⅛" outside freezer-paper edge for seam allowance (*Photo A*).

6. Clip seam allowance around inside or concave curves, making clips ¼" apart and approximately ⅛" deep. Use scissor tips to clip straight into seam allowance. Make 1 clip into sharp inside points.

7. Working with point and shank of needle, as well as your fingertips, turn under raw edge of appliqué just ahead of stitching, even with paper edge (*Photo B*). Space stitches no more than ⅛" apart, closer on tight inside corners and curves where there is little or no seam allowance.

8. Remove paper when all edges are appliquéd to background.

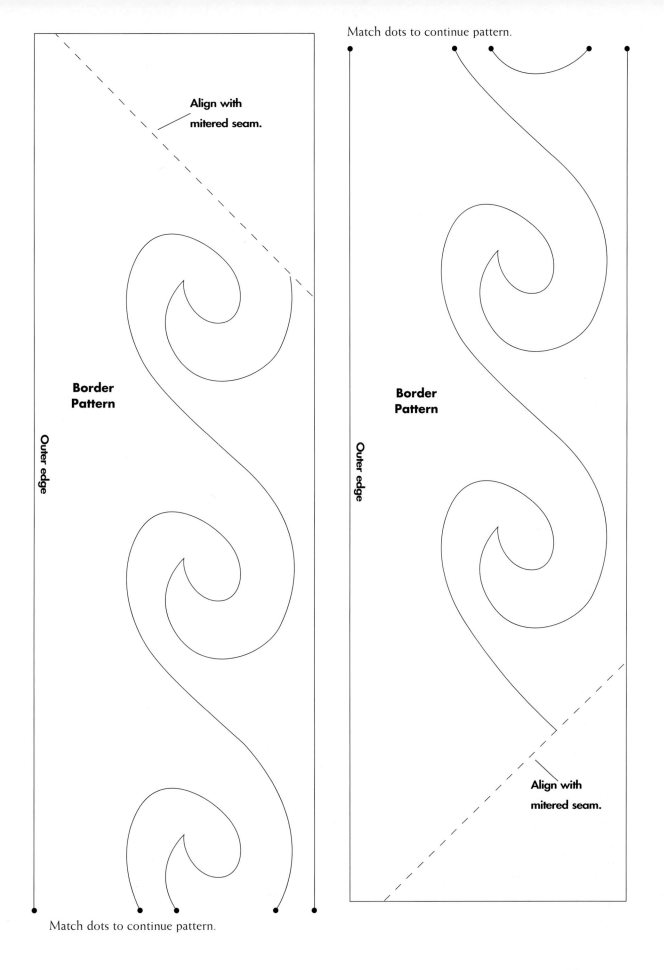

Match dots to continue pattern.

Align with
mitered seam.

Border
Pattern

Outer edge

Align with
mitered seam.

Border
Pattern

Outer edge

Match dots to continue pattern.

In the Sewing Room

taking stock

Having the right tools will increase your enjoyment of quilting and will improve your accuracy. New products are constantly appearing on the market, but below is a list of must-haves to get you started now.

cutting tools

Rotary Cutter: Buy a cutter with at least a 2"-diameter blade. The larger cutters allow you to cut through more layers. Look at the instructions on the back of the package to see the proper way to hold that brand.

Cutting Mat: Purchase the largest mat you can afford. Make sure it measures at least 18" x 24".

Cutting Rulers: Start with a 6" x 24" ruler. Later, you may want to add 6"-square, 12½"-square, 6" x 12" ruler, and triangle rulers.

Cutting Table: Select a worktable that is at a comfortable height when you stand to cut and to work. Most people prefer a cutting table that is about 36" high. There are tables available that have collapsible sides to conserve space when they are not in use.

Thread Clippers: Trim threads quickly with this spring-action tool.

Fabric Shears: A fine pair of sharp fabric shears will become a treasured possession. To keep them sharp, cut only fabric with them.

Paper Scissors: Use an inexpensive pair of large, sharp scissors to cut paper, template plastic, and cardboard—in fact, everything except fabric.

Appliqué Scissors: The extension at the bottom of one blade helps you to trim background fabrics from beneath appliqué shapes.

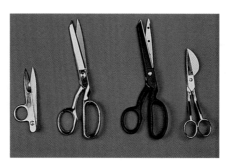

Shown from left to right: thread clippers, fabric shears, paper scissors, and appliqué scissors

sewing tools

Sewing Machine: Unless you plan to machine-appliqué, a good straight-stitch sewing machine is all you need.

Needles: Replace the needle in your sewing machine regularly. Size 80/12 is just right for machine piecing. For handwork, use a size 10 or 11 **sharp** for hand appliquéing and a 10 or 12 **between** for hand quilting.

Walking foot

Walking Foot: If you intend to machine-quilt, you must have a walking foot to feed the quilt layers through your machine evenly.

Thread: Use cotton thread for piecing and quilting. You'll find that neutral colors—white, beige, or gray—work with most quilts.

Pins: Spend a few extra dollars to get thin "quilter's pins" with small glass heads.

pressing tools

Iron: Look for a steam iron that produces plenty of steam.

Plastic Squirt Bottle: To press properly, some fabrics need a spray of water in addition to the steam from the iron.

Ironing Board: An ironing board or a large pressing pad at one end of your cutting table will enable you to stand and to press at a comfortable height.

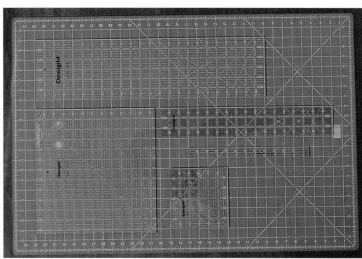

Large mat and various rulers

organizing a signature quilt

If you will be making all the blocks yourself, stabilize the signature pieces (see Step 1 of "Signing Blocks" on page 133) and distribute them to your friends. If a group of quilters will be making the blocks, refer to the block assembly instructions for the pattern you chose.

• If quilters are making blocks for you, be sure to set a theme for the quilt, whether by color or by fabric type. If you simply ask them to use their favorite fabrics, you'll end up with neons, reproduction prints, and novelty prints, and the quilt will lack cohesiveness.

• If the quilt will have a uniform background (as opposed to scrappy), buy more of that fabric than you need. That way, you can cut more pieces if some get lost or soiled.

• Purchase several Pigma™ pens (see Resources, page 144). A good choice is the .05 width. The wider tip makes writing easier and more visible.

• Decide how many blocks you need and make a list of all participants.

• Mark people off your list as the participants return their signature piece or quilt block so that you'll know who you need to follow up with.

• If the quilt will be a gift, try to use colors to suit the recipient's tastes, not yours.

adapting the quilt size

If the quilt you plan to make is not the size you want, there are several ways to adapt the design.

To make a smaller quilt, eliminate a row of blocks, set the blocks without sashing, and/or narrow the border widths.

To make a larger quilt, add rows of blocks, sashing, and/or multiple borders. Each addition requires extra yardage, which you should estimate before you buy fabric.

using our patterns

Oxmoor House patterns are printed full size. Patterns for pieced blocks show the seam line (dashed) and the cutting line (solid). Appliqué patterns *do not* include seam allowances.

making templates

Almost all of the quilts in this book can be made with rotary-cutting instructions. However, a few do require templates.

You can make templates from traditional template plastic or from cardboard. However, there is a new product that allows you to make your own templates and still use a rotary cutter to cut the fabric. Designed by John Flynn, Cut-Your-Own Templates™ are made of Formica™ (see Resources, page 144). The kit includes several sheets of Formica and everything you need to make any template shape. The Formica is thick enough that you can use your rotary cutter to cut fabric along its edge.

Cut-Your-Own Templates Kit

appliquéing

Appliqué is the process of sewing pieces onto a background to create a fabric picture.

hand appliquéing

For traditional hand appliqué, use the drawn line on each piece as a guide to turn under seam allowances. Do not turn an edge that will be covered by another piece. Hand-baste the seam allowances or eliminate basting by rolling the seam allowance under with the tip of your needle as you sew. This is called needle-turned appliqué. Pin appliqué pieces to the background.

Slipstitch appliqués to the background, using thread that matches the appliqué. (We used contrasting thread for photography purposes only.) Pull the needle through the background and catch a few threads on the fold of the appliqué. Reinsert the needle into the background and bring the needle up through the appliqué for the next stitch. Make close, tiny stitches that do not show on the right side. Remove basting when finished.

Use the drawn line as a guide.

Slipstitch around each piece.

freezer-paper appliquéing

This technique produces a mirror image appliqué piece. For directional motifs, first reverse the pattern. Then trace a full-size pattern onto the smooth (non-waxy) side of freezer paper. (Freezer paper is available in grocery stores near the aluminum foil.) Cut out each freezer-paper template along the drawn lines.

1. Press the freezer-paper template to the wrong side of the appliqué fabric.

Step 1

2. Use a special glue stick, such as GluTube® (available at quilt shops), to secure the seam allowances to the edges of the paper template. If you've ever used a glue stick with freezer paper to temporarily "baste" the seam allowances, you'll discover that GluTube works much the same way. However, GluTube is not gooey once it dries, and it will not stick to your fingers and make a mess like a glue stick can. It also allows you to create sharp, smooth edges on your appliqué. Apply the glue in a circular motion, covering approximately ¼" of the edges along both the template and the fabric. Let the glue dry for a few minutes.

Step 2

3. Cut out the template, adding ¼" seam allowance. Don't worry about cutting into the glue—once dry, it has the same consistency as the adhesive on office sticky notes.

Step 3

4. Clip curves or points as needed. Using a straight pin, fold the seam allowances over the edge of the template. Use your fingers to gently set the temporary bond. You may lift and reposition the fabric as needed.

Step 4

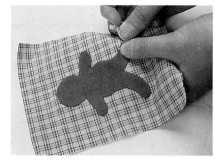

Step 5

5. Appliqué the shape to the background as usual. Clip the background fabric from behind the appliquéd shape and gently remove the freezer paper with tweezers. The template will release easily.

fusible appliquéing

If you do not enjoy handwork, fusing appliqué shapes with paper-backed fusible web may be an option for you. Follow manufacturer's instructions on the package. You will still need to cover the fabric edges so that they will not ravel when the quilt is washed. You can do this with a machine satin stitching or with hand or machine blanket stitching (*Blanket-Stitch Diagram*).

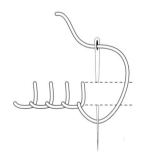

Blanket-Stitch Diagram

signing blocks

To sign blocks, you will need freezer paper and colorfast, fabric-safe pens (see Resources, page 144).

1. Before pressing the freezer paper to the fabric, use a thick-pointed permanent pen to draw a line on the paper side of the freezer paper to give you a writing guideline that will be visible through the fabric. To stabilize the fabric for writing, press the freezer paper to the wrong side of the fabric.

2. Using a colorfast, fabric-safe pen (such as Pigma™), write lightly and slowly to allow the ink to flow and to prevent the pen from catching in the weave of the cloth (fabric is rougher than paper). Let the ink dry.

3. Heat-set the ink with a hot, dry iron on the wrong side of the fabric.

Use rubber stamps for creative labels.

using rubber stamps

Stamping is a fun and easy way to add decoration and documentation to your quilts. In adapting stamping to your quilts, you are joining a historic tradition of quilt decoration. Quilters of the mid-nineteenth century used metal stamps to embellish their signature quilts.

To successfully stamp on fabric, the stamp design must be deeply etched into the rubber. Many stamps designed for paper stamping are not deeply etched. As a result, the image may be pale and the details lost on fabric. Stamps made by Susan McKelvey (see Resources, page 144) meet the depth requirements, and several of her stamps were used on quilts in this book.

Make sure that the ink you use is colorfast and fabric safe. A good choice is Fabrico™ ink, which is available in 12 colors on preinked stamp pads (see Resources, page 144).

stamping blocks

Practice on a fabric scrap to see how much ink to use and how much pressure to apply. Stamp on a hard, flat surface.

1. When inking the stamp, hold the stamp up and the stamp pad down as shown in *Photo A*. This enables you to control how much ink you put on the stamp.

2. Tap the stanp pad gently against the stamp. Press several times lightly, rather than once hard, to prevent applying excess ink.

3. Stamp the fabric by pressing firmly. *Do not* rock the stamp.

Photo A: Hold the stamp under the stamp pad while inking.

4. Let the ink dry. It dries quickly to the touch (*Photo B*).

5. Heat-set the ink with a hot, dry iron on the wrong side of the fabric.

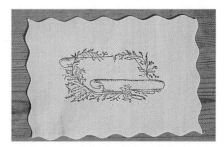

Photo B: The finished result looks professional.

using computers

If you own a home computer, try using it to print designs on your blocks and quilt labels. If you don't like your handwriting or if you just want to add some creative lettering, your computer will have a wide range of fonts from which to choose. Below is a quick review of terms to help get you started. Most of these items will be under the "Style" menu at the top of your computer screen. Because brands differ, these are only general descriptions. You will need to use your computer manual or to consult your computer dealer if you need specific information.

useful things to know

A font is the print style you use for letters. Most word processing programs come with a wide variety of fonts. Regardless of the font you choose, you can make it bold or italic, if desired.

The size determines how large your fonts will be. Normally, you don't want to use a size smaller than 10 or 12 points (pt) for the text to be read easily. Experiment to see how large you can make the letters. For a quilt label, you might consider putting the quilt's name in 36 pt; your name, date, and residence in 24 pt; and the text describing the quilt in 12 pt (see the label above).

If you have a **color printer,** you can print items in color. Be sure to run a test to see if your printer has colorfast ink; most do not. However, most black inks tend to be colorfast. Check with your computer dealer to see if colorfast ink is available for your printer.

Never use noncolorfast ink in a quilt block. However, if you choose to use it for a quilt label, be sure to print a small note in red at the bottom of the label that reminds you to remove it before laundering. A better option is to print

the design in colorfast black and then color in with Pigma™ pens.

Most computers also come with **clip art.** If not, the software is widely available (and inexpensive) at office-supply and computer stores.

You may also obtain images and fonts from the **Internet.** Download the items onto your computer. Watch for charges, though. There are many items you can download free, so only pay for those you really love. Unless you are asked to enter a credit card number, you will not be charged. Some sites allow you to download fonts free for 30 days. At the end of that time, they simply disappear from your computer.

If you own a **scanner,** your possibilities are nearly endless. Any image you can scan can be transferred to fabric.

printing on fabric

You can print what's on your screen directly onto your fabric. And you are not limited to muslin; you can use any 100% cotton fabric, as long as it is light enough for the ink to show. (*Note: Oxmoor House does not assume any responsibility for printer damage caused by trying these techniques. If your printer jams on paper, do not try to feed in fabric. Do not use these techniques at work with equipment that is not your own.*)

The quilt labels shown in this book were made on a Windows 95 compatible home PC, using an HP Inkjet 820 color printer. The text came from Microsoft Works™ for Windows 95, and the clip art is Microsoft ClipArt Gallery 2.0.

1. Design a quilt label on your screen. Enter text in your favorite font, varying the size as desired.

Photo A

Photo B

Photo C

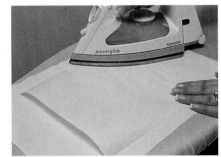

Photo D

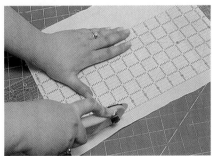

Photo E

Photo F

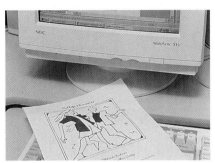

Photo G

2. Under your menu bar, find "Insert" and scroll down to "Clipart." Select the desired image and click on "OK" or "Insert" (*Photo A*). The image should now be in your quilt label text (*Photo B*).

3. Adjust text and image sizes as needed. Print a sample on paper to see if you're happy with it. Experiment to determine if your paper feeds into the printer faceup or facedown.

4. Using an old rotary cutter, cut a piece of freezer paper 8½" x 11" (*Photo C*). Using a hot, dry iron, press freezer paper to the wrong side of the fabric (*Photo D*).

5. Using your good rotary cutter, trim the fabric to 8½" x 11" (*Photo E*). Press outside edges again, to make sure the freezer paper is still secure. Check for extraneous threads along the edges and clip them, if needed.

6. Place the fabric sheet on top of the paper in your printer (*Photo F*).

7. Click on "Print." Your fabric should feed through the printer as paper would (*Photo G*).

8. Let the ink dry. Remove the freezer paper and then heat-set the ink with a hot, dry iron. Trim the image to size, if necessary.

There is a new product available called Computer Printer Fabric™ that feeds directly into your printer. Check local quilting and computer shops or order it from Connecting Threads (see Resources, page 144). The fabric is available in white and cream.

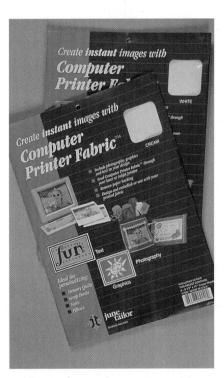

New products make printing computer images onto fabric fast and easy.

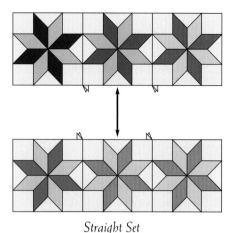

Straight Set

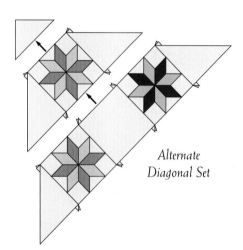

Alternate Diagonal Set

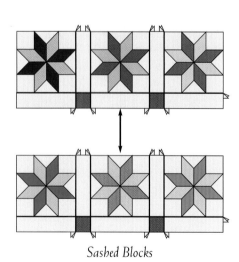

Sashed Blocks

joining blocks

Arrange blocks and setting pieces on the floor, on a large table, or on a design wall. Identify the pieces in each row and verify the position of each block. Have fun moving the blocks around to find the best balance of color and value. Don't begin sewing until you're happy with the placement of each block.

1. Press seam allowances between blocks in a straight set in the same direction. From row to row, press in opposite directions so that seam allowances will offset when you join rows.

2. In an alternate set, straight or diagonal, press seam allowances between blocks toward setting squares or triangles. This creates the least bulk and always results in opposing seam allowances when you join adjacent rows.

3. Sashing eliminates questions about pressing; just remember to always press toward the sashing. Assemble rows with sashing strips between blocks, pressing each new seam allowance toward the sashing. If necessary, ease the block to match the strip. Assemble the quilt with sashing rows between block rows.

adding borders

Most quilts have borders, which help frame the quilts. Borders can be plain, pieced, or appliquéd, with square or mitered corners.

measuring

It's common for one side of a quilt top to be slightly different from the measurement on the opposite side. Even small discrepancies in cutting and piecing add up across the quilt. Sewing borders of equal length to opposite sides will square up the quilt.

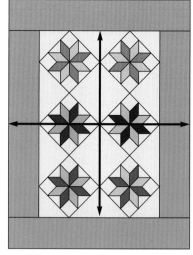

Measuring for Square Corners

When you cut lengthwise strips for borders, you'll want to measure your quilt before trimming the strips to the size indicated in the instructions. When you measure, measure down the center of the quilt rather than along the edges.

square corners

Measure from top to bottom through the middle of the quilt as shown above. Trim side borders to this length and add them to the quilt sides. You may need to ease one side of a quilt to fit the border and stretch the opposite side to fit the same border length. In the end, both sides will be the same. Unless you're using a walking foot, your sewing machine naturally feeds the bottom layer through the feed dogs faster than it does the top layer. So always put the longer side (the side that needs to be eased in) on the bottom as you sew.

For top and bottom borders, measure from side to side through the middle of the quilt, including the side borders you just added and their seam allowances. Trim the remaining borders to this measurement and add them to the quilt.

Measuring for Mitered Borders

Press the mitered corner seam flat.

mitered corners

The seam of a mitered corner is more subtle than that of a square corner, so it creates the illusion of a continuous line around the quilt. Mitered corners are ideal for striped borders, pieced borders, or multiple plain borders. Sew multiple borders together first and treat the resulting striped unit as a single border for mitering.

sewing a mitered corner

1. Measure your quilt as described in "Square Corners." Add to this measurement the width of the border plus 2".
2. Place a pin on the center of the quilt side and another pin on the center of the border.
3. With right sides facing and raw edges aligned, match the pins on the border to the quilt. Working from the center out, pin border to quilt. The border will extend beyond the quilt edges. Do not trim it.
4. Sew border to quilt, stopping exactly ¼" from the corner of the quilt top and backstitching at each end. Press seam allowance toward border. Join remaining borders in the same manner.

5. With right sides facing, fold the quilt diagonally as shown in *Mitering Diagram 1*, aligning the raw edges of adjacent borders. Pin securely.
6. Align a ruler along the diagonal fold as shown in *Mitering Diagram 2*. Holding the ruler firmly, mark a line from the end of the border seam to the raw edge.
7. Start machine-stitching at the beginning of the marked line, backstitch, and then stitch on the line out to the raw edge.
8. Unfold the quilt to be sure that the corner lies flat. Correct the stitching if necessary. Trim the seam allowance to ¼".
9. Miter the remaining corners. Press the corner seams flat.

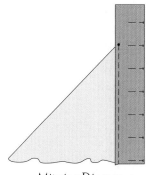

Mitering Diagram 1

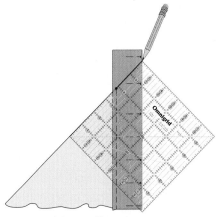

Mitering Diagram 2

preparing for quilting

The quilting design is an important part of any quilt, so choose it with care. You'll spend hours stitching together the layers of your quilt to create shadows and depths that bring the quilt to life, so make the design count.

In the "Quilting and Finishing" instructions for each project in this book, you are advised to "quilt as desired," but then you are also told how the project shown was quilted. Since most of the intricate quilting designs were from purchased stencils, the patterns cannot be reproduced within the book. Look for stencils at quilt shops.

quilting without marking

There are several ways to quilt that do not require you to mark the quilt top.
• **In-the-ditch**: Quilting right next to the seam.
• **Outline Quilting**: Quilting ¼" from the seam line. You can "eyeball" this measurement or use ¼"-wide masking tape as a guide.
• **Grid Quilting**: Quilting in straight, diagonal lines, usually 1" apart. Using the 45° line on your ruler to get you started, place 1"-wide masking tape on your quilt and quilt along its edge. Never keep the tape on your quilt for long periods of time—if you must set your project aside for a time, remove the tape.
• **Stippling**: Freestyle, meandering lines of quilting worked closely together to fill open areas.

using stencils

To find a stencil for a quilting design, check a local quilt shop or mail-order catalogs (see Resources, page 144) for one that suits your quilt.

To transfer a design to the quilt top, position the stencil on the quilt and mark through the slits in the stencil.

Connect the lines after removing the stencil.

Before using any marker, test it on scraps to be sure marks will wash out. Don't use just any pencil. There are many pencils and chalk markers available that are designed to wash out.

batting

Precut batting comes in five sizes. The precut batting listed for each quilt is the most suitable for the quilt's finished size. Some stores sell 90" batting by the yard, which might be more practical for your quilt.

Loft is the height or the thickness of the batting. For a traditional, flat look, choose low-loft cotton batting. Thick batting is difficult to quilt, unless you plan to machine-quilt or to tie your project as a comforter.

Cotton batting provides the flat, thin look of an antique quilt, making it ideal for heirloom quilts. Cotton shrinks slightly when washed, giving it that wrinkled look characteristic of all quilts. **Polyester batting** is easy to stitch and can be washed with little shrinkage. However, look for the word "bonded" when selecting polyester batts. Bonding keeps the loft of the batt uniform and reduces the effects of bearding (migration of loose fibers through the quilt top). Avoid bonded batts that feel stiff.

Layering a quilt

backing

The instructions in this book tell you how to cut and to piece standard 42"-wide fabric to make backing. The backing should be at least 3" larger than the quilt top on all sides.

For a large quilt, 90"- or 108"-wide fabric is a sensible option that reduces waste and eliminates backing seams. Quilters are no longer limited to muslin; new wide fabrics are available in lovely prints.

Some quilters treat the backing as another design element of their quilt, choosing to piece interesting designs or to appliqué large shapes.

layering

Lay the backing right side down on a large work surface, such as a large table, two tables pushed together, or a clean floor. Use masking tape to secure the edges, keeping the backing wrinkle-free and slightly taut.

Smooth the batting over the backing; then trim the batting even with the backing. Center the pressed quilt top right side up on the batting. Make sure the edges of the backing and the quilt top are parallel.

basting

Basting keeps layers from shifting during quilting. Baste with a long needle and white thread (colored thread can leave a residue on light fabrics). Or use safety pins, if you prefer.

Start in the center and baste a line of stitches to each corner, making a large X. Then baste parallel lines 6" to 8" apart. Finish with a line of basting ¼" from the edge.

Some quilters use nickel-plated safety pins for basting. Pin every 2" to 3". Don't close the pins as you go, as this can pucker the backing. When all pins are in place, remove the tape at the

Thread basting

quilt edges. Gently tug the backing as you close each pin so that pleats don't form underneath.

Pin basting

Another popular method is to use a basting gun, which shoots plastic tabs through quilt layers. Use paper-cutting scissors to cut the tabs away after the quilting is done.

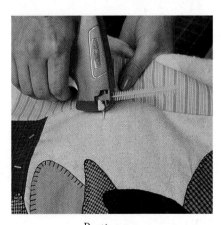

Basting gun

quilting

Quilting is the process of stitching the layers of a quilt together, by hand or by machine. The choice of hand or machine quilting depends on the design of the quilt, how much time you have, and the quilt's intended use. The techniques differ, but the results of both are functional and attractive.

hand quilting

To make a stitch, first insert the needle straight down (*Photo A*). With your other hand under the quilt, feel for the needle point as it pierces the backing. With practice, you'll be able to find the point without pricking your finger.

Roll the needle back as far as you can

(*Photo B*). Use the thumb of your sewing hand and the hand underneath to pinch a little hill in the fabric as you push the needle back through the quilt top. Gently tug the thread to pop the knot into the quilt. Then rock the needle back to an upright position for the next stitch. Load 3 to 4 stitches on the needle before pulling it through.

With 6" of thread left, tie a knot close to the quilt top. Backstitch; then pop the knot into the batting. Run the thread through the batting and out the top to clip it.

machine quilting

If you plan to machine-quilt, you must have a walking foot or an even-feed

presser foot for your sewing machine to allow all the quilt layers to feed through your machine evenly (*Photo C*). Use the same foot for straight-line quilting.

For free-motion quilting or stippling, you will need a darning foot (*Photo D*). Lower the feed dogs or cover them. You control the stitch length by manually moving the fabric.

Another option is to hire someone who owns a professional quilting machine to quilt your project. Check your quilt shop or guild for local sources.

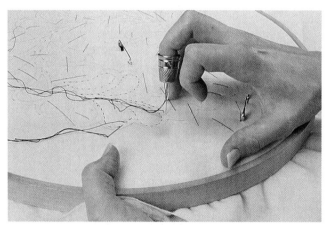

Photo A

Photo C

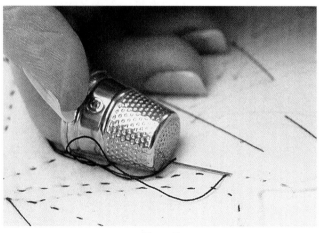

Photo B

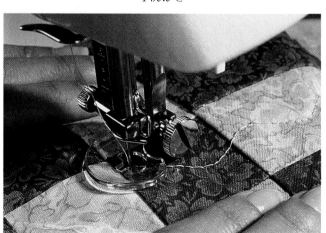

Photo D

binding

A quilt must have bias binding when it has curved edges or rounded corners. If you use a plaid for the binding and want the plaid to appear "on point," use bias binding. For all other situations, use straight-grain binding.

making straight-grain binding

1. Cut needed number of strips selvage to selvage. Cut strips 2¼" wide when working with thin batting and 2½" wide when working with thicker fabric (such as flannel) or batting.
2. Join strips end to end to make a continuous strip. To join 2 strips, layer them perpendicular to each other, with right sides facing. Stitch a diagonal seam across strips as shown in *Diagram A*. Trim seam allowances to ¼" and press open.
3. Fold binding in half lengthwise, with wrong sides facing. Press.

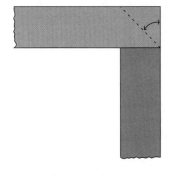

Diagram A

adding binding

Sew binding to the front of the quilt first by machine. Begin stitching in the middle of any quilt side. Do not trim excess batting and backing until after you stitch the binding on the quilt.
1. Matching raw edges, lay binding on quilt. Stitch binding to quilt, using ⅜" seam and leaving about 12" unstitched at the top (*Diagram B*).

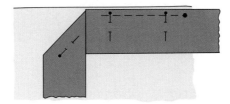

Diagram B

2. Continue stitching down side of quilt. Stop ⅜" from corner and backstitch. Remove quilt from machine and clip threads.
3. Fold binding strip straight up, away from quilt, making a 45° angle (*Diagram C*).

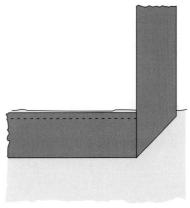

Diagram C

4. Fold binding straight down along next side to be stitched, creating fold that is even with raw edge of previously stitched side.

5. Begin stitching at top edge of new side (*Diagram D*). Stitch length of new side. Continue until all 4 corners and sides are joined in this manner. Stop stitching ¼" from point where binding began. Trim excess binding, leaving a 12" tail. Join the 2 tails with diagonal seams (*Diagram E*). Trim excess binding beyond diagonal stitching and press open. Stitch a straight line (as usual) over this area to secure the ¼" open space (*Diagram F*).

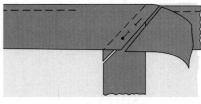

Diagram D

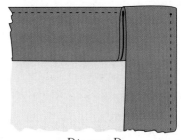

Diagram E

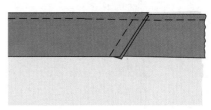

Diagram F

6. Trim excess batting and backing even with binding raw edge.
7. Turn binding over raw edge of quilt and slipstitch in place on backing with matching thread. At each corner, fold binding to form a miter. Whipstitch miter closed. (The miter should form naturally when you turn the corners to the back of the quilt.)

making bias binding

Step 1

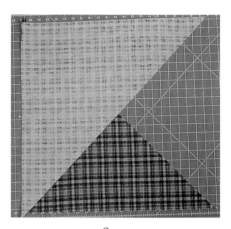

Step 2

Step 3

1. To cut bias binding, start with a square. (For a queen-size quilt, a 32" square is sufficient.) Center pins at top and bottom edges, with heads toward inside. At each side, center a pin, with head toward outside edge.

2. Cut square in half diagonally to make 2 triangles.

3. With right sides facing, match edges, with pin heads pointed to outside. Remove pins and join triangles with a ¼" seam. Press seam open.

Step 4

Step 5

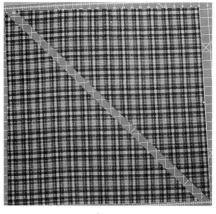

Step 6

4. On wrong side of fabric, mark cutting lines parallel to long edges. Space between lines would equal the width of the desired strip (for example, 2¼").

5. Match edges, with pin heads pointed to inside and right sides facing, offsetting 1 width of binding strip as shown. Join edges with a ¼" seam to make a tube. Press seam open.

6. Begin cutting at extended edge. Follow drawn lines, rolling tube around as you cut, until all fabric is cut into a continuous strip. See instructions on page 141 for adding binding to quilt.

quilt labels

Every quilt you make should include a quilt label. You can appliqué or piece the label to the back, or include the information in a quilt block on the front.

At a minimum, your quilt label should include:

• The name of the quilt
• Your name
• Your city and state
• The date of completion or the date of presentation

Additional information can include the story behind the quilt, the maker, and/or the recipient. Consider recording how old you were when you made the quilt.

There are numerous ways to embellish your quilt label. Look for ideas within this book or use your computer (see page 134) to find images. Rubber stamps are fun to use, too (see page 133).

You can add more labels if the quilt is displayed, published, or acknowledged with an award.

Even if you purchase an antique quilt, make a label. Research the pattern to see if you can determine the approximate date the quilt was made or simply write "unknown." But at least put your name and the date and the place you purchased it for future reference.

multiple labels

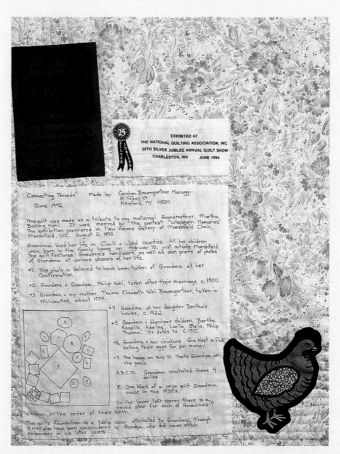

Some quilts feature multiple quilt labels. In this example, the quiltmaker started out with a detailed label explaining all the images featured on the front and the stories behind them. Then, as the quilt was exhibited, won awards, and was published, she added more quilt labels. Each label represents an important part of the quilt's history. Future owners will appreciate knowing how the quilt's fame progressed. Just for fun, the maker also appliquéd a chicken to the back.

This quilt label explains how the quilt evolved from a thirtieth birthday party. The signature blocks on the quilt front convey much of the story, but the maker wanted to tell about her birthday party and why she chose the pattern she did for the blocks. She used computer clip art to make the festive image across the top and entered text in the "Party" font below. When she was satisfied with the image on-screen, she printed it onto computer printer fabric.

Resources

Computer Supplies
CompUSA Inc.
Over 200 computer superstores nationwide

CompUSA Net.com Inc.
Online computer superstore for Internet sales
www.compusanet.com

General Quilt Supplies
Contact the following companies
for free catalogs.

Connecting Threads
P.O. Box 8940
Vancouver, WA 98668-8940
1-800-574-6454

Fons & Porter Quilt Supply
P.O. Box 171
Winterset, IA 50273
1-800-985-1020
www.fonsandporter.com

Hancock's of Paducah
3841 Hinkleville Road
Paducah, KY 42001
1-800-845-8723
fax (502) 443-2164
www.Hancocks-Paducah.com

Keepsake Quilting™
Route 25B, P.O. Box 1618
Centre Harbor, NH 03226
1-800-865-9458
www.keepsakequilting.com

Photo Transfer
Photos-To-Fabric™
Mallery Press
4206 Sheraton Drive
Flint, MI 48532-3557
1-800-278-4824
www.quilt.com/amisimms

Rotary-Cutting Rulers and Mats
Omnigrid, Inc.
1560 Port Drive
Burlington, WA 98233
(360) 757-4743

Rubber Stamps, Pigma™ Pens, Ink
Wallflower Designs
Susan McKelvey
P.O. Box 307
Royal Oak, MD 21662
Send $3.00 for catalog.

Template Material
Cut-Your-Own Templates
Flynn Quilt Frame Company
1000 Shiloh Overpass Road
Billings, MT 59106
1-800-745-3596
www.flynnquilt.com